"BE·MUCH OCCUPIED WITH JESUS"

SEA HARP PRESS

Endorsements

In a world where the lines between right and wrong are becoming more and more blurred, where wrong has become right and right has become wrong, it is time for courage and boldness. It is far easier to let someone else take the risk, but I think we are all called to say to the Lord, "here I am, send me."

This book is about exactly that.

Tom Lehman
PGA Player of the Year
Ryder Cup Captain
British Open Champion

Looking For The One reminds us that the way to change the world is to start with one person at a time. But before looking for the one, we look to Jesus. Because Jesus is the only one who can change us and heal us, we go to Him first. Jesus is the way, the truth, and the life!

Rod Carew
Minnesota Twins, California Angels
7 American League Batting Titles
18 Time All Star
American League MVP
MLB Hall Of Fame

How amazing is it to personally know Jesus and be able to share with others who are hurting, lost, and discouraged that they too can have a close relationship with the Savior who will never leave them or forsake them? *Looking For The One* is an inspiring book of true stories of lives that have been changed forever through the faithfulness of David McIver. His passion to find those in need and share Christ is evident and I believe this book will inspire many to do the same!

Matt McPherson
CEO Mathews Archery, Inc. & McPherson Guitars, Inc.;
The Salvation Poem Foundation: Director / Co-Author

I felt inspired and challenged after reading David's book. Encounter after encounter, he walks you through conversations that lead to lives being changed. I am thankful to call David a friend. You will enjoy his storytelling but it's his practical application of sharing the gospel that we can all learn from.

Derek Green
Hobby Lobby / HL Investments

"There's got to be more!" That's what my wonderful Christian friend said to me. He believes all the beliefs. He goes to all the meetings. He serves in the church. But he's restless for "more." Maybe like you. The elusive "more" is accepting Jesus' invitation to join Him in the greatest Cause on the planet— "to seek and save the lost."

Cue the "Mission Impossible" music. Telling people about Jesus is one of the great "I should's" of following Jesus. And, sadly, one of the great "but I don't's." So many fears. So many questions. For many of us, it seems like the scariest obedience of the Christian life.

David McIver's *Looking for the One* makes helping someone be in heaven so doable! He takes sharing Christ out of the clouds and embeds it in in our "everyday"— auto repairs, recreation, banana bread, little emergencies, eating out. These stories of real people sharing and encountering Jesus in real life are inspiring and emboldening— and just plain heartwarming.

This book shows us a lifestyle that makes our high-stakes "Mission Impossible" into "Mission Possible." And makes your "everyday" into something that will matter forever. It's the "more" you've been restless for! As you join your Jesus in *Looking for the One*.

Ron Hutchcraft
Veteran radio host, author and spiritual rescue coach

Dave is one of those people who can spark up a conversation with anyone and then make that person (whether they are a friend or total stranger) feel like that conversation is the most important thing going on in Dave's life! And that is because to Dave, it is! He has a special way of connecting with people, and he uses that to share the love of Jesus with others. I was fortunate to have Dave as my in-season pastor while playing for the Twins, and I have heard some of these amazing stories already! I was excited to hear he was writing this book about *Looking for the One* because I knew it would be filled with sound Bible teaching, contain applicable ways to grow in your faith, and help you find ways to bring up Jesus more in your everyday conversations. Dave is always trying to live out the verses in Luke 15 about leaving the 99 to find THE ONE, and I know you will enjoy reading about some of those people that have encountered Jesus because Dave said yes to this mission!

Kyle Gibson
MLB pitcher:
Twins, Rangers, Phillies, Orioles
2021 Major League All-Star

The stories in this book have propelled our family's faith in a new and exciting way as we are *Looking for the One* each day. These are the messages and the stories the world needs to hear! For David McIver, in the year 2016, I was the one.

Kurt Suzuki
MLB catcher:
Athletics, Nationals, Twins, Braves, Dodgers
2014 Major League All-Star
2019 World Series Champion

Looking for the One is an amazing book. My friend, David McIver, has the unique gift of finding The One, that person God brings in his life who needs to meet Jesus. You'll be inspired by God's appointments. And you'll be moved by David's ability and availability to get right down to that one person's need. And you will be motivated yourself to be aware of the One that God brings to you each day. What a difference it would be in the world and in the church if we each were *Looking for the One.*

Wayne Pederson
Leader of Reach Beyond; Senior Leadership at Moody Broadcasting, NRB, CMB, and Northwestern Media (KTIS)

Over the years, I have had the privilege to witness firsthand how God uses David's life and ministry to impact lives worldwide. *Looking for the One* is a powerful reminder that all believers are empowered to reach people for God. If you want to follow the example Jesus set forth and find practical means to share the Gospel in relational and transformative ways, this is the right book for you.

Rob Hoskins
President, OneHope

If you want to learn how to effectively share the love of Jesus with others, *Looking for the One* is a must-read! The power of the Gospel exudes through the pages as David McIver narrates a series of short, inspiring stories about life-changing encounters that win souls for Christ. This book is a great reminder of how each of us can become more like Jesus when we look to share His love with others.

Charlie Ward
Former NBA athlete & Heisman Trophy winner

Every page of *Looking for the One* reflects David McIver's deep love for Jesus, his trust in Holy Spirit to lead him to the lost and lonely, and his desire to share a faith that transforms lives.

The day David changed his prayers and asked Jesus what was on His heart, he started receiving waves of personal revelation that empowered him to reach out to the people he encountered every day.

Looking for the One is not merely a collection of inspirational stories, but a practical guide for you to change how you share your faith. Leading questions, equipping tools, and reflection prompts will encourage you to apply the principles David shares.

This book will encourage you to listen more closely to Holy Spirit's promptings and to be obedient to His instructions. As you start seeing the life-changing results of your prayers, you too will be motivated to look for 'the one' who needs to experience the love and forgiveness of the Lord. Just ask Jesus who is on His heart? Like David, you will discover that it is a simple prayer, but it will change your life.

Graham Power
Founder Global Day of Prayer & Unashamedly Ethical

LOOKING
for the
ONE

*Stories of Seeing the
Lost, Lonely, and Broken
Through the Eyes of Jesus*

DAVID McIVER

To all the messengers with beautiful feet—

"But how can they call on him to save them unless they believe in him? And how can they believe in him if they have never heard about him? And how can they hear about him unless someone tells them? And how will anyone go and tell them without being sent? That is why the Scriptures say, 'How beautiful are the feet of messengers who bring good news!'" (Romans 10:14-15)

To my wife Sherrie—

Thank you for loving me and speaking God's Word into this book. I thank Jesus for the day I looked over at you in church and began to fall in love!

CONTENTS

INTRODUCTION

> *"The numbers are staggering, and they break your heart. More than 2 billion have never heard the name of Jesus, and 70,000 die each day without Christ."*
>
> **Alliance For The Unreached**

> *"A few weeks ago I was speaking to a friend about evangelism and he shared a statistic that shocked me! Apparently less than four percent of Christians will ever share their testimony with another person in a meaningful and intentional way during their lifetime."*
>
> **Transform Your Work Life, Graham Power and Dion Forster**

AT SOME POINT, you've been encouraged to share the gospel. After all, "How can they believe in him if they have never heard about him?" (Romans 10:14) After listening to a missionary, you may have run out the door with a handful of gospel tracts or driven home feeling uncomfortable. You may have felt guilty or pressured.

In Sunday School, I learned that I should share my faith. We sang "This Little Light of Mine" over and over. As a teenager, I went door to door with a youth pastor who got into several heated arguments with strangers. In my twenties, there were a handful of opportunities to share my faith, but most years there were no opportunities and a whole lot of guilt. I was on track to join the majority of Christians who rarely share the gospel in their lifetime.

But all of that changed one day. My friend Tim called, and after lying facedown before the Lord, his plan was simple. His goal each day was to look for the one. It might be a financial need, a cup of cold water, or the gospel, but Tim had surrendered his schedule to Jesus. He believed that God was big enough to take care of his business and bring him one person each day. I could hear the excitement in Tim's voice. It was so simple.

One A Day.

In Luke 15 Jesus makes it simple: "Suppose one of you has a hundred sheep and loses one of them—what do you do? You leave the other ninety-nine sheep in the pasture and go *looking for the one* that got lost until you find it. When you find it, you are so happy that you put it on your shoulders and carry it back home. Then you call your friends and neighbors together and say to them, 'I am so happy I found my lost sheep. Let us celebrate!' In the same way, I tell you, there will be more joy in heaven *over one sinner who repents* than over ninety-nine respectable people who do not need to repent" (Luke 15:4-7, GNT, italics mine).

I know what you are thinking. Your schedule is crazy, or you've tried to witness but it didn't go well. Someone asked a question, and you didn't know what to say.

Let's start with your schedule. My friend Tim is busy. I have sat in his office and watched him navigate a blizzard of phone calls and questions from his team. But when Tim goes looking for the one, time stands still. Tim believes in his heart of hearts that lost and hurting people are more important than his schedule. He believes that God's bottom line is more important than his bottom line.

Several years ago, Tim called, and instead of one opportunity to share Jesus, there were seven "appointments" in one day. Seven! I was never a straight-A student in high school, but on this day, I got it. When Tim stops to help someone, that "delay" is life-changing. The delay is also a timing mechanism for setting up the next appointment. Each act of obedience leads to arriving on time for the next meeting. And when the dust settles, God can open doors and bless our bottom line in ways that our selfish efforts cannot. "He takes no pleasure in the strength of a horse or in human might. No, the Lord's delight is in those who fear him, those who put their hope in his unfailing love" (Psalm 147:10-11).

How about the questions that you can't answer? Not having all the answers means that you have to depend on the Holy Spirit. Your dependence is what God desires in looking for the one. Because you don't have all of the answers, you instinctively see these encounters as relationships instead of talking points. Instead of theological or political debates, all you want to talk about is Jesus.

These short stories are not a system or a program. This is abiding with Jesus and his heart for the lost people in your life. The broken, the forgotten, the abused and the outcasts. It's about your family members who need to experience Jesus. It's the adventure of seeing strangers meeting Jesus.

Reading these short stories takes only five minutes a day, but I have a prediction. During the next month, you'll start to think differently:

> The delay at the airport? "Yes! The one is on my flight!"
>
> The angry co-worker? "Jesus, this anger is really an open door to their heart."
>
> The single mom serving your table? "Lord, may this extravagant tip be an expression of your love."

The week you have to spend in the hospital? "Someone in that hospital needs to know him!"

The family member who wants nothing to do with Jesus? "Jesus, show me their heart."

There are times it takes years to develop a relationship, but most of the time looking for the one happens in daily moments of obedience. It might only be a trip to the grocery store, but you walk into this store as a representative of Jesus. "So we are Christ's ambassadors; God is making his appeal through us. We speak for Christ when we plead, 'Come back to God!'" (2 Corinthians 5:20)

Looking for the one is life-changing, but the first life to be changed is yours.

Because as you look for the one, you become like the One.

You become more like Jesus.

HOW JESUS LOOKED FOR THE ONE

"Peter and John won the crippled beggar, and his transformed life led to the conversion of two thousand people! Like Jesus, the apostles took time for individuals" (Warren Wiersbe).

Let's imagine an earlier scene in John, Chapter 4, involving those same two: As the torchlight flickers across the walls, you look around the room. James and John are in deep conversation, and Peter is gesturing with his arms as he tries to convince Andrew of something. You smile as you look into each face. These are your friends. These are your brothers.

You are gathered because the Master has decided that it is time to leave Judea and return to Galilee. More importantly, he has decided to walk through Samaria. You wonder to yourself if Samaria is just a shortcut to Galilee, or is Samaria somehow part of the master's strategy? Because of the tensions between the Jews and Samaritans, the stakes are high.

Now you turn and look at Jesus.

Jesus is seated at the head of the table, and he is looking from face to face. As his eyes meet your eyes, time stands still. No more random thoughts. No more questions. His gaze captures your heart. His calm gathers your calm.

The next day is a long walk, and as you pass through Samaria you reach Jacob's well. Now it is time to go into the village to buy food. But you see the weariness on the face of Jesus. It is time for Jesus to rest at the well. As you enter the village, you are surrounded by Samaritans. As you buy food, you wonder if Jesus is planning to reveal to this village that he is the Messiah.

In returning, you see the well in the distance, and it looks like someone is talking to Jesus. As you come closer, your questions turn to shock. Jesus is talking to a Samaritan woman. This is so unthinkable that you join a circle of disciples who are speechless.

Suddenly, this woman leaves her water jar beside the well and begins running to the village. Within minutes, the villagers are streaming out to see Jesus.

Jesus did not hold an organized meeting or connect with the leaders of the city, but he did have a plan:

The plan was to ask a sinful woman for a drink of water.

Jesus spoke to large crowds. But over and over, we see him looking for the one. He takes time for children, lepers, tax collectors, and fishermen. When Jesus healed the sick, sometimes he spoke a word while other times he spit on the ground. When it is time to reach an entire village, he looks for a sinful woman and asks her for a drink of water. He knows all about her sin, but he looks for her. He chooses her.

Jesus could have ridden into the village on a stallion. He could have arranged for his followers to carry him on their shoulders like royalty. But Jesus takes a long dusty walk so that a weary woman can see his weariness. He becomes thirsty so that her thirst can be quenched. Jesus goes on a journey that is costly to him. "Jesus, tired from the long walk, sat wearily beside the well about noontime" (John 4:6).

As Jesus comes to set her free, he humbles himself and invites her into a relationship. He gently says, "Please give me a drink" (John 4:7). When she hesitates, we hear the heart of Jesus. "If only you knew the gift God has for you and who you are speaking to, you would ask me, and I would give you living water" (John 4:10).

We hesitate to help a stranger or share the gospel because we see ourselves at the story's center. How will they respond to me? Will the gospel break our relationship? But as we look into the face of one who is lost, it is not about a relationship with us. It is a relationship with Jesus.

We become fearless as we whisper the words of Jesus, "If only you knew."

The one you are speaking to is trying to quench their thirst with things that can never satisfy their heart. They need to know the difference between water that cannot satisfy and water that is a well-spring of life. Jesus made it clear. "Anyone who drinks this water will soon become thirsty again. But those who drink the water I give will never be thirsty again. It becomes a fresh, bubbling spring within them, giving them eternal life" (John 4:13).

The Samaritan woman responds to Jesus with the words you hear when looking for the lost. "Please give me this water!" (John 4:15)

Because of Jesus, someone is set free from sin and shame and understands why their Father is looking for them. "But the time is coming—indeed it is here now—when true worshipers will worship the Father in spirit and in truth. The Father is looking for those who will worship him that way. For God is Spirit, so those who worship him must worship in spirit and in truth" (John 4:23-24).

A.W. Tozer sheds some light on why Jesus came and why he looked for the lost. "Why did Christ come? Why was He conceived? Why was He born? Why was He crucified? Why did He rise again? Why is He now at the right hand of the Father? The answer to all these questions is, 'In order that he might make worshippers out of rebels'" (*Experience God in Worship*, as quoted by John S. Miller).

As this sinful Samaritan woman meets the unconditional love of Jesus, she begins to run. She is not running from Jesus but running to share Jesus. "The woman left her water jar beside the well and ran back to the village, telling everyone, 'Come and see a man who told me everything I ever did! Could he possibly be the Messiah?' So the people came streaming from the village to see him" (John 4:28-30).

HOW JESUS LOOKED FOR THE ONE IS HOW WE LOOK FOR THE ONE.

We go on long walks that test and try us.
We become thirsty so that we connect with the thirsty.
We ask:
>What is your name?
>Why are you anxious?
>What are you looking for?
>Do you believe this?

We watch as eyes open in wonder.
We rejoice as someone begins to run.

If we believe that looking for the one is a life of weariness, Jesus speaks life to us. "My nourishment comes from doing the will of God, who sent me, and from finishing his work" (John 4:31-34).

As Jesus sees a sinful woman, he invites his followers to wake up and look around. "You know the saying, 'Four months between planting and harvest.' But I say, wake up and look around. The fields are already ripe for harvest. The harvesters are paid good wages, and the fruit they harvest is people brought to eternal life. What joy awaits both the planter and the harvester alike! You know the saying, 'One plants and another harvests.' And it's true. I sent you to harvest where you didn't plant; others had already done the work, and now you will get to gather the harvest" (John 4:35-38).

Henry Blackaby beautifully summarizes the encounter at the well: "We try to teach evangelism to Christians, or how to witness as kingdom citizens. Evangelism is not a program. It is a by-product of a healthy, growing, vibrant relationship with Jesus Christ as Lord. Jesus did not have to teach the woman at the well how to witness. He redeemed her, and she brought the whole city to see the man who changed her life!" (*The Man God Uses*)

As we walk with Jesus, we dare to believe the words of Jesus:

"The Spirit of the Lord is upon me,
for he has anointed me to bring Good News to the poor.
He has sent me to proclaim that captives will be released,
that the blind will see,
that the oppressed will be set free,
and that the time of the Lord's favor has come" (Luke 4:18-19).

As we walk with Jesus, we see the lost, lonely, and broken through his eyes.

Looking For The One
WHO NEEDS TO TASTE AND SEE

"Jesus. You should seek nothing more, you should settle for nothing less. You need Jesus—not some creed, code, or cause. You don't go beyond Jesus. You may go deeper into Jesus, but you'll never go beyond Jesus. The table is set. Come and dine."

Adrian Rogers

"THERE IS BANANA BREAD in the refrigerator." Ed and Sylvia have a cabin with a beautiful view and a kayak on the shore. More importantly, Sylvia stocks the refrigerator with the necessities of life. It had been several years between visits, and as I drove north, I was looking forward to catching some bass. I had set aside time to be with Jesus and begin writing this book.

After a quiet morning of worship and writing, it was time for a lunch break. I made a smoothie, and after all of that healthy food, it was time for dessert. After all, man does not live by smoothie alone. As I watched the butter melting into the bread, I began to watch the carpenter who was working at Ed and Sylvia's.

When I handle power tools, it's not a pretty picture. I spend most of the time figuring out a plan of attack or fumbling with the equipment. This guy knew what he was doing. There were no wasted movements and no hesitation. I strolled outside to compliment the craftsman and ask about his pickup truck. Nothing profound, just some guy talk amid the odor of sweat and sawdust.

When I came back inside, the Holy Spirit gently spoke. "Bring Jason a slice of banana bread." I've lost count of the times when I receive an impression, and my first response is to analyze the impression. Since I was spending a day with Jesus, there was no analysis. Just simple obedience.

Now it was time for a quick warm-up in the microwave. I went for a double portion slice and then thought of Sherrie's admonition. "Everything's better with butter."

When I walked outside, Jason was sitting in his truck eating his lunch. We talked for a few minutes about his carpentry business, but there was no prompting to talk about anything spiritual. He shared that Ed and Sylvia had told him that I was working on a book, so he was trying to keep the noise levels down.

By mid-afternoon, it was time to stop writing and start paddling. I floated down the shoreline casting a spinner-bait with no depth finder and no idea where to fish. When I arrived at a small bay, the bass were waiting for me. Then I hooked a nice northern pike, which almost capsized the kayak. As I paddled back to the cabin, I could see someone standing near the shoreline. The odd thing was that this person was standing like a statue and looking in my direction.

It was Jason.

When I arrived on shore, Jason asked for a moment. When we met at lunchtime, Jason shared that he had recognized my voice from listening to the radio station for which I work. "I didn't say anything about knowing that you are a pastor, but I began to think about my childhood when you went inside. I thought about what it was like when my dad, a pastor, left my mom. I remembered all of the talk in our small town about my family. As I sat in the truck, all of the pain started to come back. I remembered walking away from the Church and God. I remembered all of the family members who walked away from God.

"About that time, I looked up, and you were offering me a piece of Sylvia's banana bread." There was a long pause as we listened to the waves lapping against the shore. Jason cleared his throat, and then his voice was firm.

"When I took the bread, I felt the love of Jesus...

"As I felt his love, I felt drawn to him again."

I thanked Jason for sharing something so personal, and I had an impression at that moment. "Jason, as you are sharing, I am getting a picture of a wall surrounding you. I feel like you've been told that you have to break through the wall. That you need to take it apart brick by brick. But I think that Jesus is holding out his hand and offering to lift you over the wall."

Then we prayed to the God who has been lifting us for generations. "He lifted me out of the pit of despair, out of the mud and the mire. He set my feet on solid ground and steadied me as I walked along" (Psalm 40:2).

When I finished praying, Jason shared that a friend had been telling him repeatedly that there was a wall he needed to break through. But Jason said, "I just haven't known where to start, and I haven't had the energy to figure it out." I could see the relief on Jason's face as he thought about Jesus lifting him over what he could not tear down.

A few days later, I received a text from Jason that he has graciously given his blessing to share with you:

> David, thanks for the kind message and prayer. This
> morning I wrote down the events that day at the cabin,
> how God revealed something I didn't even know was

there, and how he used a simple act of kindness by a man who was trying to find some time to write a book.

Banana bread of all things! God is just so creative and kind. I'm in tears just thinking about it. He's just so good! Also, I love how God saw fit to honor Sylvia's generosity in providing bread for her guests by using it for his secret and beautiful purposes. Thank you for your kindness. You have no idea how large 'the wall' has loomed in my life. I have been feeling new courage as a result of recent events. Bless you!

Jason is right. Jesus works in secret and beautiful ways.

Jesus has been watching Jason for decades, interceding for him. Now Jesus whispers to Ed and Sylvia to hire Jason. When I ask if I can use their cabin to write a book, Sylvia begins to bake bread. As Jason sits in his pickup truck, remembering all of the pain and betrayal, he breathes in the aroma of bread. He breathes in the love of Jesus. The name of the lake where Jesus touches his heart? Battle Lake.

The next day I called Sylvia. "I gave some of your bread to Jason, and and he felt the love of Jesus." I loved the laughter in her voice as she said, "Praise the Lord!"

All of this so that Jason can taste and see again that the Lord is good.

REFLECT:

Which neighbor needs to taste and see the goodness of the Lord?

Who can you invite into your home?

EQUIP:

How do I look for the one who needs to taste and see?

PRACTICE HOSPITALITY: When you invite people into your home, you are practicing biblical hospitality. When you create a meal or bake bread, the aroma of Jesus greets them at the door. When something goes wrong with the meal, it's because you are not called to perfection. You are called to practice hospitality. "When God's people are in need, be ready to help them. Always be eager to practice hospitality" (Romans 12:13).

DOOR TO DOOR: When my wife, Sherrie, sees a moving truck in our neighborhood, she pulls out her recipe for chocolate chip cookies. The night before the next-door neighbors move away, Sherrie orchestrates cookies and sparkling cider to thank them for their friendship. Then we pray over them.

HE WILL LIFT: If relationships wear us out, it is because, at some point, we have taken on the responsibility of fixing someone's life. We have taken on a responsibility for their decisions. But our only role is to love people and bring them to Jesus. His role is described in Psalm 27: "For he will hide me in his shelter in the day of trouble; he will conceal me under the cover of his tent; he will lift me high upon a rock" (Psalm 27:5, ESV).

UNHEALED PAIN: I recently heard from Jason, who reminded me that tasting and seeing is not a one-time experience. Jesus miraculously rescued Jason at age 19 and continues to reach him in the midst of unhealed pain and struggles. Jason's summary of his heart touches my heart. "Jesus walks with us through the process and loves us into healing, by whatever means he chooses. Like kindness shown through a plate of hot buttered banana bread. I'm a struggler who was saved and yet in need of healing."   Someone in your world is struggling and needs to taste and see that the Lord is good.

LET'S PRAY:

Jesus thank you for opening my eyes, and giving me ears to understand. Thank you for the aroma of salvation in my life. Please open my eyes to the one who needs to taste and see that you are good. I open my home to your presence, and I open my door so that someone has a place at your table.

DISCUSS:

Were you raised in a home that practiced hospitality?

What is the atmosphere like in your home when you have guests?

"Show hospitality to one another without grumbling" (1 Peter 4:9, ESV).

What is your language of love? What kind of kindness do you love to receive?

How does hospitality pave the way for an encounter with Jesus?

"Taste and see that the Lord is good. Oh the joys of those who take refuge in him!" (Psalm 34:8)

Why does Jesus describe himself as "The bread of life"?

"I am the living bread that came down from heaven. Anyone who eats this bread will live forever; and this bread, which I will offer so the world may live, is my flesh" (John 6:51).

As I look for the one who needs to taste and see, how do I become more like Jesus?

2

Looking For The One
WHO NEEDS A COACH

*"The heart of salvation is the Cross of Christ. The
reason salvation is so easy to obtain is that it cost God
so much. The Cross was the place where God and sinful
man merged with a tremendous collision and where
the way to life was opened. But all the cost and pain
of the collision was absorbed by the heart of God."*

Matt Redman

I FELL IN LOVE with golf at Peters Sunset Beach as a teenager.
My main job was to mow the rough and run a weed whacker. My
favorite job was the early morning trip around the course to empty
the garbage containers. Almost every day, there was something that
took my breath away. I would pause as a deer bounded down the
fairway or to see the beauty of flowers in the first light of day.

By the way, my love of golf had little to do with my ability to play
golf. I managed to cobble together a rusty set of irons, but with no
lessons, golf was an endless series of bad shots.

My wife, Sherrie, and I were blessed with three sons, and each of
the boys took turns whacking at plastic golf balls in our yard. As the
boys grew older, they demonstrated an interest in golf and worked
odd jobs that helped us purchase used equipment. We gradually

began to acquire various golf gadgets by carefully watching eBay. We installed a net in our garage, and as I held golf books by David Leadbetter, Jack Nicklaus, and Ben Hogan, I began to coach the boys. Within a few months, the boys started to win Junior PGA events.

As I coached the boys, I quietly longed for someone who would coach me. Then one day, I met Roger Kuhlmann. Roger was a successful tournament player, and his daughter Barb had played for years on the LPGA tour. My first lesson from Roger was in the driving rain. He changed my grip and set up. Then suddenly it happened. I struck a nine iron and heard Roger's beautiful laugh. "You've never done that before, have you?" The answer was, "No!" That day was the beginning of a life-changing friendship, and golf became the avenue for Roger to coach me in every area of life.

As Roger coached me, I began to look for people to coach. I still remember the day a young lady from Germany was in tears as she was trying to hit irons on the driving range. As a transfer student, she was new to the golf team and embarrassed to shank ball after ball in front of her teammates. I knew her coach and asked if I could lend a hand. I spoke to her in German and English, and within a few minutes, her friends gathered around as she began to hit seven irons over 150 yards. They even applauded her!

In August of 2003, a golf course in Brainerd called The Legacy held a grand opening weekend. Members of the media were invited to try out the course and include any three guests of their choosing. I asked the boys to be my guests, and they jumped at the chance.

It was a gorgeous day with scenery that was off the chart. As we made our way through the back nine, we came to the 13th hole. This hole is a 321-yard dogleg par four, and I knew that I had hit my drive well. The problem was that it was well right of my target line. There is an old saying: "Don't complain about a shot while it is in the air." This is sage advice. As I watched my tee shot, I murmured that I had missed my target by 20 yards.

We arrived at the hole and searched the rough and deep grass in front of the green. My Strata 4 golf ball was nowhere in sight. After a while, Jordan asked, "Do you want me to check the hole?" "Sure—we have nothing to lose."

"Dad, there's a golf ball in the hole. It's a Strata 4." There was nothing to do but begin the celebration! There are times when we have to leave our kids at home and spend the day with clients or donors. But on this day, the arms that hugged me belonged to the ones I love the most.

Getting a hole-in-one with your sons is terrific. Still, my favorite golf memory is a lesson I gave to a construction worker. We were alone on a driving range, and as we shook hands, I felt the iron grip of his calloused hands. As he began to hit golf balls, the ground thudded as he lunged at the ball. Awkward swings were followed by muttering under his breath. He could cuss with the best of them.

When you are looking for the one on a golf course, you pray some bold prayers. "Jesus—help me figure out this golf swing so quickly that this man knows it's you. Reveal yourself in a golf lesson."

A reverse pivot happens when a golfer moves away from the ball at impact. The result is inconsistent contact and a "flipping" motion at the bottom of your swing. As I watched the lunging motion and dirt spraying into the air, somehow I knew what was wrong and how to fix it. I prayed, took a deep breath, and asked Dick if he would be open to a swing change. I explained the reverse pivot and how to adjust his swing so that he was moving through the ball at impact.

Within seconds Dick's weight was on the inside of his right foot. Then I moved his strong hands ahead about two inches in front of the ball. Then I prayed as he drew the club back.

When you look for the one, you get a front-row seat as God pursues lost people. You see the look in their eyes when they begin to sense the love of Jesus. In this case, I saw the look in Dick's eyes as he flushed an iron with a beautiful draw. It couldn't be possible, but ball after ball landed by the flag.

It was quiet on the driving range as Dick turned to me. "What made you come over to me?"

"Dick, when I saw you standing there trying to figure out your golf game, I sensed that you've had to figure out a lot of things on your own. I got a glimpse of how hard your life has been." Dick pushed his cap back and slowly nodded. He began to share what it's like to work day after day when you're tired and worn out. He talked about the aches and pains. Then I sensed it was time.

"Dick—As you may have noticed, golf is almost impossible to learn on our own. We need someone to see what we cannot see. We need a coach because we are better together." I explained to Dick that I work in Christian radio and that my greatest joy is to see people go from having heard about God to knowing him for themselves.

"In my spiritual life, I have guys who coach me. They see things that I can't see, and they have my back. I know we just met a few minutes ago, but if you would like to know God and have your own relationship with him, I would be honored to talk about that."

Dick's reply was classic. "Let's go!"

I love visuals, so I took four of my clubs and laid them on the ground at 90-degree angles about three feet apart. I explained that the clubs illustrated the great divide between God and us. I shared that our sins separate us from a holy God and that no matter how hard we try, we can't get from one side to the other. The best of us and the worst of us are in the same boat. "For everyone has sinned; we all fall short of God's glorious standard" (Romans 3:23).

Dick slowly nodded.

"Now, Dick, I need your driver and a seven iron...

"On our own, we have no chance to get from one side to the other. We've already blown it. But God made a way. He sent his son Jesus to die in our place and pay the price for our sins." I laid down Dick's clubs in the shape of the Cross, with the seven iron covering the area over the great divide.

"Dick, the only way we can make it to God is to cross over on the Cross of Christ. Today, you can accept his death for you. You can trust your life to him and begin to follow him. You can be forgiven of every sin."

Dick slowly raised his head.

"That's the most beautiful thing I've ever heard. How come no one has ever told me that before?"

Dick removed his cap, bowed his head, and gave his life to Jesus.

REFLECT:

Is there an activity or hobby that refreshes me?

Is this activity a connecting point with someone who needs a coach?

EQUIP:

How do I look for the one who needs a coach?

ENJOY LIFE!: Recreation is a gift of God and opens the door to relationships that matter.

INVEST IN PEOPLE: As you invest in someone's success, the Holy Spirit opens their heart to receive Jesus.

BE CONFIDENT WHEN FACING OVERCONFI-
DENCE: The ones acting like they have all the answers
are often the ones most in need of a friend.

ASK FOR PERMISSION: Your gentle invitation to
share about Jesus may be what they secretly desire. As
you speak of Jesus, you can see it on their face. "How
come no one has ever told me this before?"

RECKLESS ABANDON: I know. Sharing the gospel is
risky. Rejection is never easy to receive. But, I want you
to notice something. Spend time with someone sold
out for Jesus. Looking at their face, you see joy because
they have seen the face of Jesus. "I have one desire. To
live a life of reckless abandon for the Lord, putting all
my energy and strength into it" (Elisabeth Elliot).

LET'S PRAY:

*Jesus, I know that any sport or activity can take over my life
or become a distraction. But I also know that the things I
enjoy are connecting points to people's hearts. Help me to
enjoy activities, but only worship you. Help me to invest in
people so they can cross the great divide to you.*

DISCUSS:

How can an activity put the gospel into action?

*"And I am praying that you will put into action the
generosity that comes from your faith as you understand*

and experience all the good things we have in Christ"
(Philemon 1:6).

When is a hobby no longer refreshing us but becoming a distraction?

How would you communicate and illustrate the gospel to someone you are coaching?

Do I see sharing my faith as awkward, or is it a privilege to receive eternal life?

> *"We can see that God has also given the Gentiles the privilege of repenting of their sins and receiving eternal life"* (Acts 11:18).

As I look for the one to coach, how do I become more like Jesus?

3

Looking For The One
WHO NEEDS A
SECOND CHANCE

"Christ came to earth for one reason: to give his life as a ransom for you, for me, for all of us. He sacrificed himself to give us a second chance."

Max Lucado

ONE OF MY FAVORITE WAYS to connect with Jesus is to end the day by talking to him. I ask him to show me the day from his perspective. Often he brings to mind a small moment of obedience that pleased his heart. In those moments, he convicts me or encourages me.

I used to end almost every day feeling like a failure, but now I end my day just talking to Jesus. He knows that I stumble and fall, and yet he loves me!

In March of 2018, I flew from Minneapolis to Fort Myers, and as I was falling asleep afterwards, I asked Jesus about my day. I immediately sensed his still, small voice: "The woman next to you on the plane, she doesn't know me, and I wanted you to talk to her." I felt the conviction of the Holy Spirit. I thought back to taking my seat and thinking that I had too much to do. I was too tired to look for the one.

I could picture the older woman seated next to me, and I had helped with her bag. We had introduced ourselves to each other, and I remembered that her name was Pat. I had mentioned that I worked in Christian radio. But my non-verbals must have been clear. I was not interested in a conversation.

I asked forgiveness for not speaking to her. Then as I drifted off to sleep, I asked Jesus if he would give me a second chance to share the gospel with Pat. I know—what a ridiculous prayer. But think about it for a moment. If the God of the Universe wants you to share the gospel with someone, is it absurd for him to move heaven and earth to give you a second chance?

The next day was one of those beautiful Florida days with not a cloud in the sky. I arrived at Hammond Stadium for a Twins game and joined over 8,000 people streaming into the stadium. As I reached the main concourse, I looked up and did a double-take. The older woman walking in front of me looked like the woman from the plane. Could it be? Over the din of the crowd, I said, "Pat, is that you?!"

She stopped. She turned around. Then I saw her smiling face. After a word of greeting, I opened with, "Pat, I want to apologize for being such a poor company on the flight."

She said, "I had hoped to talk to you, but I could see that you were busy."

I am not sure how Jesus does this, but suddenly it seemed like we were the only two people standing in the concourse. Even the noise around us seemed to fade.

"Pat, what was it that you wanted to talk about?"

"When I was a little girl, our family went to hear Billy Graham. As he gave the invitation to come forward, I wanted to go but felt I wasn't good enough. That was over fifty years ago. Since then, I've never felt like the good in my life outweighed the bad. I've always wondered what I should do."

I gave Pat a copy of the Salvation Poem and then shared the good news from Romans 5:8: "But God showed his great love for us by sending Christ to die for us while we were still sinners." In other words, because of Jesus, it's not about the good outweighing the bad. While we were still sinners, he gave his life for our sins.

I briefly shared, "God saved you by his grace when you believed. And you can't take credit for this; it is a gift from God. Salvation is not a reward for the good things we have done, so none of us can boast about it" (Ephesians 2:8-9).

I held Pat's hands as she bowed her head and accepted Jesus as her Savior. After waiting for so many years, her eyes opened, and joy radiated to every part of her face. Then, I realized the rest of the story.

"Pat, do you know what is happening at this exact moment?"

"No."

"You mentioned that over 50 years ago, you went to a Billy Graham crusade. His funeral is taking place right now. Of all the times when you could have given your life to Christ, Jesus chose this time."

Billy's funeral was on March 2, 2018, and we laughed together at the thought that now Pat would be able to thank him in person for planting the seed of the gospel all those years before.

At that moment, Pat's son walked up and noticed that his mom had been crying. "Mom, are you okay?" As they walked away, I heard Pat say, "Something just happened that I want to tell you about."

I stood there, overwhelmed with the presence of God. He answered my prayer! Then it occurred to me: *Jesus had given both of us a second chance.*

REFLECT:

Where do I need a second chance?

Do I feel like a disappointment to God?

EQUIP:

How do you look for the one who needs a second chance?

TALK TO JESUS: If you end almost every day feeling like a failure, close your day by talking to Jesus. He knows that you stumble and fall, and yet he loves you! He will convict you of sin, but he will also remind you of even little moments of obedience. You will not fall asleep listening to "the one who accuses them before our God day and night" (Revelation 12:10).

RECEIVE YOUR FREEDOM: As you are set free from condemnation, you are prepared to set someone free from accusation. You have someone in your life that goes to sleep thinking that they are a failure. They believe that the good in their life will never outweigh the bad. You may have tried to encourage them or share the good news of Jesus. You may have given up any hope of reaching them. Perhaps what they need is a revelation of the grace of God.

ASK FOR A SECOND CHANCE: The God of the universe can arrange their schedule or change their heart so that they are ready to receive the gift of salvation. I believe that you will see their eyes radiate with joy as they understand the price that Jesus paid to set them free.

LET'S PRAY:

Jesus, I confess that I have listened to the accuser instead of listening to you. Speak your life to me. I open my heart to your conviction and your encouragement. Now I ask that you show me the one who feels like a failure. If I have missed an opportunity to reach out to them, I ask for a second chance! Please help me to look for the one! I don't want one person to miss knowing you. I don't want one person to wait fifty years to give their life to you.

DISCUSS:

What are some of the things Satan accuses you of at the end of the day?

Has anyone ever given you a second chance?

Do you feel God is disappointed in you?

Where do you need a second chance?

In the story of the prodigal son, how does Jesus reveal the heart of the Father?

"So he returned home to his father. And while he was still a long way off, his father saw him coming. Filled with love and compassion, he ran to his son, embraced him, and kissed him. His son said to him, 'Father, I have sinned against both heaven and you, and I am no longer worthy of being called your son.'

"But his father said to the servants, 'Quick! Bring the finest robe in the house and put it on him. Get a ring for his finger and sandals for his feet. And kill the calf we have been fattening. We must celebrate with a feast, for this son of mine was dead and has now returned to life. He was lost, but now he is found.' So the party began" (Luke 15:20-24).

How do I become more like Jesus as I give someone a second chance?

4

Looking For The One
WHO HAS QUESTIONS

"The gospel must be preached afresh and told anew to every generation, since every generation has its own unique questions."

Helmet Thielicke

"CAN I SEE YOU for a minute?" I looked up and tried to hide my surprise. This member of the Twins was a great guy but not someone I had spoken to at length before. He had never even attended one of our chapel services.

I followed him out to the dugout, and as we sat down, I thought we might warm up with a conversation about baseball or the weather. This guy got right down to business. "I want you to know why I don't attend chapel. At an early age, my parents told me that God creates people knowing in advance which ones will go to hell. So, in essence, he is creating people to punish them forever. Is that true? Because if it's true, then I don't want anything to do with a God like that."

In moments like this, I am guided by James 1:19: "Understand this, my dear brothers and sisters: You must all be quick to listen, slow to speak, and slow to get angry." In other words, even if I have a great answer at the tip of my tongue, if I speak too quickly, I might miss the real reason for the conversation. In this case, the question about hell was the tip of the iceberg. As I asked questions, I began to see a man with a passion for justice and a heart for people.

As the conversation unfolded, something else was happening. The dugout was filling up with guys waiting to take the field, and several of his teammates sat down to listen in. Whether it is a kitchen table, a boardroom, or a dugout, people all around us are repelled by arguments but drawn to conversations. If we are quick to listen, slow to speak, and slow to get angry, we have a more effective platform to declare the truth of God's Word.

The other advantage of being slow to speak is that it gives you time to pray! Eventually, I asked a question. "On your wedding day, were you there because you had to be there or fell in love?" He answered, "I fell in love." "Now, imagine that God told you that you had no choice but to love him? Would that really be love?" Jesus invites us to love him, knowing that we might refuse him. Jesus said in John 16:9: "The world's sin is that it refuses to believe in me."

We talked about freedom to choose God and then turned to the mystery of God's sovereignty in the book of Ephesians. "Even before he made the world, God loved us and chose us in Christ to be holy and without fault in his eyes. God decided in advance to adopt us into his own family by bringing us to himself through Jesus Christ. This is what he wanted to do, and it gave him great pleasure" (Ephesians 1:4-5).

The dugout was quiet as I shared an illustration from my days as a Bible major at Bethel College. I remember one of our professors describing the scene at the gates of heaven. As we draw near, we see the words etched above the gate. "Whosoever will may come." As we enter the gate and look back, we read, "Chosen before the beginning of time."

The mystery is that both are true.

Now it was time to ask a question. "Because we can choose to love Jesus, we can choose to reject him. So the biggest question is this: are you willing to choose to love Jesus? Are you willing to follow him?"

He said, "I'm in," and we left the dugout. That Sunday, he walked into chapel for the first time.

As you encounter questions, I believe that most people are looking for two things: an answer and a relationship. This is why I try to build a relationship before attempting to answer a question. When we have no idea what to say, we take heart from what an old preacher once said as he pointed up: "He's in management, and I'm in sales." When asked about something like physical healing, I am reminded of what one of our announcers from Africa shared: "I am careful never to take the place of God."

There are other times when the only response to a question is to say nothing. I recall the day a farmer stopped by our PraiseLive studio in Osakis, Minnesota, and asked if he could see me for a few minutes. Because I grew up on a farm, his heavy work boots and coveralls were familiar sights. As we sat down, he began to cry. Then he began to weep. As he gained his composure, he shared about the day that he was cutting wood with his sons. There was an accident, and one of his sons was crushed under a falling tree. As he drove his son at high speed to the hospital, he lost control of the vehicle. This accident took his other son's life.

As his pain and questions poured out, there was nothing to say. His tears said it all. I wrapped my arms around him and held his pain close to my heart.

As Jesus walked on the earth, he welcomed our questions and held our pain. After the death of Lazarus, when Jesus finally arrives four days later, Martha greets him with, "Lord, if only you had been here, my brother would not have died" (John 11:21). Jesus answers her grief and "if only" with a life-changing declaration. "I am the resurrection and the life. Anyone who believes in me will live, even after dying" (John 11:25). As Lazarus comes forth, "if only" is replaced with a revelation of the glory of God.

> I lay my "whys?"
> Before your cross
> In worship kneeling,
> My mind beyond all hope,
> My heart beyond all feeling;
> And worshipping,
> Realize that I
> In knowing You,
> Don't need a "why?"
> (Ruth Bell Graham)

Our only hope is to bring our questions to the resurrection and the life of Jesus. Our questions are holy ground as we lay them at the foot of the cross.

REFLECT:

Have I brought my questions to the foot of the cross?

Who do I know that is looking for an answer and a relationship?

EQUIP:

How do I look for the one with questions?

ASK QUESTIONS: Jesus was asked a question about his authority, and he responded with a question. "Let me ask you a question first" (Luke 20:3). Your questions signal that your heart is open to their heart.

GOD'S WORD: Because God's Word is living and active, read it cover to cover. As you study this Word, the Holy Spirit can bring it to mind during any conversation. If you are more of an introvert than an extrovert, try looking at questions as a game of catch. Someone has just tossed you a question, and they are looking to see if you are willing to throw the ball back to them. Be patient. You will know when it is time to present the truth of God's Word. You'll know when they "catch" it!

WEATHER THE STORM: You know that person who loves to provoke you? When it seems like questions are really an attack, remember these words from Warren Wiersbe: "So often those who are intensely wrong as lost sinners become intensely right as Christians and are greatly used of God to win souls" (Warren Wiersbe).

THE EMPTY TOMB: Questions provide insight and are open doors for interaction. But when you reach a roadblock, the empty tomb is greater than any question. "Through Christ you have come to trust in God. And you have placed your faith and hope in God because he raised Christ from the dead and gave him great glory" (1 Peter 1:21).

INVITE TO TRUST: Questions are part of exploring our faith, but at some point, we move from questions to trust. "You love him even though you have never seen him. Though you do not see him now, you trust him; and you rejoice with a glorious, inexpressible joy. The reward for trusting him will be the salvation of your souls" (1 Peter 1:8-9).

LET'S PRAY:

Jesus, as we live in this broken world, we encounter broken people. Their questions break our hearts. Please give us wisdom when to listen, when to speak, and when to hold them close to our heart. When questions are beyond our reach, help us lift their eyes to you.

DISCUSS:

What are some of the questions you have wrestled with regarding your faith?

Have any of these questions been a connecting point as you share Jesus?

How does this passage speak to the question of free choice and predestination?

"As for us, we can't help but thank God for you, dear brothers and sisters loved by the Lord. We are always thankful that God chose you to be among the first to experience salvation—a salvation that came through the Spirit who makes you holy and through your belief in the truth. He called you to salvation when we told you the Good News; now you can share in the glory of our Lord Jesus Christ. With all these things in mind, dear brothers and sisters, stand firm and keep a strong grip

on the teaching we passed on to you both in person and by letter.

"Now may our Lord Jesus Christ himself and God our Father, who loved us and by his grace gave us eternal comfort and a wonderful hope, comfort you and strengthen you in every good thing you do and say" (2 Thessalonians 2:13-17).

What is our part in salvation?

How do you respond to questions about God's sovereignty?

How do you discern if there is a question behind a question?

As you look for the one with questions, how do you become more like Jesus?

5

Looking For The One
WHO NEEDS TO STAND UP

"As my grandmother was passing away she suddenly looked up and said, 'There's Jesus.' Then she was gone. Are you ready to stand before Jesus?"

Billy Graham, Chicago Crusade 1962

THE CALL FROM PANAMA brought everything in our world to a screeching halt. "Tyler is on his way to a hospital. His fever is over 105 degrees."

Our son Tyler was on a mission trip to Panama with Teen Mania, and as a 14-year-old, was a long way from home. We had very few details, but from the brief phone call we knew that Tyler was in serious trouble.

As we hung up the phone, I was ready to spring into action. There had to be someone that we could call. But my wife Sherrie spoke a better word. "Before we go to the phone, let's go to the throne." We knelt beside our couch and began to pray. We cried out for healing and that somehow a doctor would bring Tyler's fever under control.

As we prayed, I suddenly remembered a conversation with a business leader a few weeks before. As he shared about his business interests in Central America, I shared about Tyler's upcoming Panama trip. For some reason, he wrote down a name and a number and said, "If your son gets into a medical situation, you need to take him to the Johns Hopkins hospital in Panama City. It is brand-new and state of the art. Here is my contact person for the hospital."

Moments later, we were on the phone to Panama with a team member who was in the cab with Tyler. As the call connected, they pulled up to an old clinic in a rough part of town. When I shared my connection with Johns Hopkins, the cab driver said that the hospital was less than a mile away. Because of that moment on our knees, Tyler was being driven to a state of the art hospital.

You know how medical battles ebb and flow. One moment the news is all good, and then moments later, the word is all bad. The news at first was good. In light of this, I decided to keep my commitment to speak to the men at Prairie Correctional Facility in Appleton, Minnesota. One of the PraiseLive radio stations is KCGN, and the 100,000-watt signal reaches this prison. We had received many testimonies of how the programming had resulted in salvation and changed lives through the years.

The drive to the prison is about an hour, and as I was on the outskirts of Benson, Minnesota, Sherrie called. She had just received a phone call from Panama, and the news was not good. Tyler was fighting for his life. As I sat on the edge of the road, we asked Jesus if I should turn around and go home. The Holy Spirit spoke to both of us. "Go and minister to the men at the prison."

Going through multiple gates and razor blade fences is always sobering to me. But when the men came into the chapel room, I was uneasy. You could feel the tension in the air. As they sat down, I noticed the men dividing into distinct racial groups. The room was restless and agitated, and when the prisoner leading the service tried to get their attention, there was no drop in volume. Finally, there was just enough break in the noise, and the men could hear him speak.

"Guys, our speaker tonight is David from PraiseLive. Many of you know his voice from 101.5 FM. What you don't know is that David's son is in Panama on a mission trip, and tonight, David's son is fighting for his life." The room grew quiet. "David and his wife got the call a few minutes ago, and he still chose to come and be with us." Now you could hear a pin drop. "Before he speaks, I want all of us to pray for Tyler."

Now a ripple of prayer spread through the room. Then a tidal wave of prayer.

I shared about Tyler's battle for his health and the news we had just received. I spoke of my deep love for Tyler. Then I set my notes aside and shared why knowing Jesus is a matter of life and death. I shared that I would give anything to take Tyler's place and even give my life for him. Then I shared John 3:16, "For this is how God loved the world: He gave his one and only Son, so that everyone who believes in him will not perish but have eternal life." The message was so brief and so simple, and yet the presence of God was everywhere.

I invited the men to close their eyes and bow their heads. Then I asked anyone who wanted to invite Jesus Christ to forgive their sins to raise their hands. There were almost 100 men in attendance, and 28 raised their hands. I prayed over the men and offered program guides for PraiseLive, and even Bibles that they could pick up on the way out.

My heart rejoiced!

As the men left the room, four of the leaders came and formed a semi-circle around me. It was more like a complete circle. These were four huge men who loved Jesus. The leader got right to the point. "You didn't do us any favors tonight. These men who raised their hands are now walking back to their cells, and they are all alone. They are under attack, and we don't know who they are. We can't follow up on them if we don't know who they are."

I remember the many times that I heard Billy Graham share the gospel and explain why he was about to invite you to come forward. Billy explained that when Jesus asked people to follow him, over and over, it was an invitation to make a public stand for him.

The next day, I connected with Tyler in his hospital room, and I shared what happened when the men heard about his condition. I shared about the men crying out for his healing. Then I shared about the 28 decisions for Christ. Tyler responded, "Then it's worth it all."

As Tyler made a full recovery, I thought about the wave of prayer in that prison. It was holy ground to witness those prisoners fighting for my son's freedom.

Several months later, I was invited back to Prairie Correctional, and as I greeted the men, I thanked them for the night they prayed for Tyler. I shared how his life was hanging in the balance and my belief that their prayers had turned the tide in Tyler's favor. Once again, I shared the gospel, and as I closed the meeting, I told them about my last visit. I shared what their leaders had said after the meeting.

"Tonight it's going to be different. I want every eye open. If you want to surrender your life to Jesus, in a moment, I am going to ask you to stand up. I am asking you for a public decision for Christ, so that your brothers in Christ can encourage you and stand beside you. But before you stand up, I have a word for the guys around you who are already walking with Christ. When your friend and brother stands up, I want you to raise the roof. We yell and scream for home runs and touchdowns, but I want you to let these guys hear it. I want you to join the celebration taking place in heaven.

"Now, if you are ready to surrender to Jesus, and turn your life completely over to him, stand up!"

There were a few seconds where no one moved. Then one man in about the third row stood to his feet. The room erupted. Then a guy in the back stood to his feet. He was greeted with shouts and slaps on the back. Then all over the room, men were standing to their feet. Now almost every man in the room is shouting and stomping and high-fiving the new believers. I asked the guys to circle up around the ones who had dared to take a stand and to pray over them.

As I drove home in the moonlight, I thought about the sound of prayer as brothers cried out for each other. I thought about the words of Jesus, "Everyone who acknowledges me publicly here on earth, I will also acknowledge before my Father in heaven" (Matthew 10:32).

I thought about the new followers of Jesus. Alone in their cells but surrounded by their brothers.

REFLECT:

Have I ever made a public declaration of faith in Christ?

Who do I know that needs to take a stand for Christ?

EQUIP:

How do I look for the one who needs to stand up?

COUNT THE COST: We oftentimes think that we need to downplay the cost of following Jesus. In Matthew Jesus made it very clear: "If you refuse to take up your cross and follow me, you are not worthy of being mine. If you cling to your life, you will lose it; but if you give up your life for me, you will find it" (Matthew 10:38-39).

LOVE LIKE JESUS: To love someone is to love them enough to speak the truth. Dietrich Bonhoeffer gave his life for the gospel and he makes the connection between receiving the love of Jesus and then seeing with the love of Jesus: "There is now no time to lose: the work of harvest brooks no delay. 'But the laborers are few.' It is hardly surprising that so few are granted to see things with the pitying eyes of Jesus, for only those who share the love of his heart have been given eyes to see. And only they can enter the harvest field."

DISCERN THE MOMENT: There are times when you quietly share Jesus and invite people to respond privately. But there are also times when the Holy Spirit makes it clear. This gathering is a line in the sand, and it is time for a public declaration for Christ. There are times when healing happens in private. There are other times when Jesus says to our brokenness, "Come and stand in front of everyone" (Luke 6:8). In the case of a prisoner who has just been set free, their life may depend upon being rooted in community.

LET'S PRAY:

Jesus, forgive me for the times I have been afraid to stand up for you. Wash away my past and grant me a new boldness to witness for you. As I share the gospel, I ask for wisdom in providing an opportunity to respond. If you are working in the quiet and hidden places, I honor your work. If you desire to be at the center of a room that is stomping and shouting for joy, I say, "Yes!"

When people all around me are bowing down to worship the world, give me the courage to stand up for you. Though choosing you may enrage those who are in authority, keep me steadfast. So engulf me in your love, O Lord, that my heart would break before it would dishonor you.

DISCUSS:

How does boldness overcome opposition?

"Yet our God gave us the courage to declare his Good News to you boldly, in spite of great opposition" (1 Thessalonians 2:2).

When someone threatens us, who are they really threatening?

"And now, O Lord, hear their threats, and give us, your servants, great boldness in preaching your word" (Acts 4:29).

How does boldly entering God's presence give us boldness to speak for him?

"Because of Christ and our faith in him, we can now come boldly and confidently into God's presence" (Ephesians 3:12).

How do you know when it is time to invite a public declaration of Christ?

Have you ever given an invitation to Christ and no one responded?

"For I am not ashamed of this Good News about Christ. It is the power of God at work, saving everyone who believes— the Jew first and also the Gentile" (Romans 1:16).

How do I become more like Jesus as I invite people to take a stand?

6

Looking For The One
ALONE IN THE DARK

*"But my life is worth nothing to me unless I
use it for finishing the work assigned me by the
Lord Jesus—the work of telling others the Good
News about the wonderful grace of God."*

Acts 20:24

IT WAS LATE, we were tired, and as we neared our home, we saw something that made no sense. Pedaling along, in the dark, was an older woman. She was wearing a dress with a purse over her shoulder. There were no lights on her bicycle and no reflective markers on her clothing. The speed limit was 50 MPH, and there were almost no streetlights to guide her.

But of course, it was late, and we were both weary. We spoke for a moment about the circumstances that would lead someone to be so alone in the dark. I could hear uneasiness in Sherrie's voice. Something was wrong.

There are times when looking for the one is almost effortless. The right person appears at the right time, like picking a piece of ripe fruit. There are other times when looking for the one takes effort. It is the work of telling others the Good News about the wonderful grace of God.

I found a place to turn around, and within moments we saw her. She was standing at a street corner, looking up at road signs. I carefully introduced myself, and it quickly became apparent why she appeared to be confused. She spoke almost no English, but her face communicated fear and exhaustion. I asked Jesus how to help her.

I noticed her iPhone and pantomimed, "Can you make a phone call?" She pointed at her phone and shook her head no. Then the helper, the Holy Spirit, gave an insight. I showed her the contacts on my phone, and as I pointed from my phone to her phone, I asked if there was someone I could call.

I love it when the Holy Spirit helps us. I saw the instant recognition on her face as she paged through her contacts and then pointed at a cell number. I dialed the phone number.

I can still remember the frantic sound of a young lady's voice. Her panic turned to joy when I explained who I was standing next to on the street corner. "We've been looking for Mom for hours." As I hand my phone to her mother, I understand none of their conversation. But the look on her face is priceless. One moment she is alone in the dark, and the next moment she hears the sound of one she loves. Hope replaces fear and exhaustion.

It turns out that Mom had just arrived from China. With no ability to communicate in English and a cell phone not activated to work in the United States, she decided to ride a bicycle to a family member across the city. She had been lost and alone for hours. I gave her mom our contact information and a copy of the Salvation Poem. I explained to her daughter that we work in Christian radio and, as followers of Jesus, were honored to help her mom.

One of the beauties of meeting people worldwide is the traditions and cultures we experience. As we were about to leave, the beautiful woman in the dress began to speak to us and bow to us. Her words of blessing washed over us. I clasped my hands in front of me and bowed to her. As we bowed to each other, I prayed that Jesus would take the experience of going from lost to found and turn her heart to him.

The next day, Sherrie received a text message from a daughter who loves Jesus and had been trying to share Jesus with her mother. Now her mom discovered that the people who found her in the dark are followers of Jesus! Sherrie directed the daughter into a Bible Study Fellowship group in the days that followed.

I can still see her pedaling in the dark when I close my eyes. Then I remember my overseas trips and times I felt alone and lost. As a teenager, my cousin Bob and I became lost at night in the city of Jerusalem and, at one point, stumbled into a family gathering. We were strangers in a strange land. As I imagine her pedaling hour after hour, I wonder if she was afraid to ask for help. Or was she determined to find her family on her own? How many times had she asked for help?

Now I imagine Jesus watching her. Jesus sees her fear and is filled with compassion. As her good shepherd, Jesus is looking for someone to look for her. We are not qualified to speak her language, but we are willing to be available. Jesus orders our late-night schedule to see her through his eyes and carry his love to her. Moments like this are why God commands us to love one another!

"Dear friends, since God loved us that much, we surely ought to love each other. No one has ever seen God. But if we love each other, God lives in us, and his love is brought to full expression in us" (1 John 4:11-12).

Would you like to become more like Jesus? Begin by receiving his love and inviting him to live within you. Then as you walk with Jesus, his love becomes a natural extension of your life. As you express the love of Jesus, he transforms you.

Because as you look for the one, you become like the One.

You become more like Jesus.

REFLECT:

Who do I know that is alone in the dark?

EQUIP:

How do I look for the one alone in the dark?

LOOK IN THE DARK: The person assigned to you doesn't know the language of heaven, and they don't know who to trust. They can't find their way home. They are alone, exhausted, and beginning to lose hope. As your heart begins to break, submit your schedule to Jesus. Be willing to look around or turn around even when you are tired.

In the 1990s, PraiseLive invited Ron Hutchcraft to our listening area in Minnesota, and there were over 500 decisions for Christ. Months before the weekend, we held a meeting for pastors, and Ron asked if we could agree on two things: People all around us are lost; lost people need Jesus.

In the silence, Ron asked us to close our eyes and to picture the face of someone in our life that does not know Jesus. Then he asked us to look into their eyes. There were months of prayer and hard work, but the reason for that wave of salvation was that as we closed our eyes, Jesus opened our eyes and broke our hearts.

ACCEPT YOUR ASSIGNMENT: I remember homework assignments from high school and college. The assignments were necessary, but there were times I was not intentional enough to finish them. In other words, I was lazy and unmotivated.

When it comes to telling the Good News of Jesus, there is far more at stake than a grade point average. Paul shares that this is an assignment given directly by Jesus. How important is this assignment to Paul? "But my life is worth nothing to me unless I use it for finishing the work assigned me by the Lord Jesus—the work of telling others the Good News about the wonderful grace of God" (Acts 20:24).

If you say "Yes" to the work that Jesus has assigned to you, then someone alone in the dark will receive an expression of the love of Jesus!

LISTEN TO HIS VOICE: Take time to listen to his voice. There are times when turning around is not his will. There are other times when it is his assignment. Jesus said, "My sheep listen to my voice" (John 10:27).

EXAMINE YOUR HEART: Someone in the dark may look different than you. Is there any critical spirit or prejudice that would hinder you from seeing someone through the eyes of Jesus?

PREPARE TO BE REFRESHED: During seasons when you feel weary, think about the last time you helped someone. You were tired, but because of your obedience, they were ministered to, and you were refreshed. "The generous will prosper; whoever refreshes others will be refreshed" (Proverbs 11:25).

LET'S PRAY:

Jesus, I gladly say "Yes" to this assignment! Instead of focusing on me, I focus on the one. I submit to your authority in my life. I yield my heart to your heart and my schedule to your priorities. I am willing to listen to your voice and look through your eyes. Purify and prepare my heart. When I don't know what to say, I trust you to give me your words. As I turn around in the dark, I look for the one on your heart.

Thank you for this assignment. Thank you for refreshing me!

DISCUSS:

Who did Jesus describe as lost?

"For the Son of Man came to seek and save those who are lost" (Luke 19:10).

What is the price of being lost?

"If you receive Him it will be well; if you reject Him and are lost it will be terrible" (D.L. Moody).

What is the heart of Jesus for someone alone in the dark?

"The people who sat in darkness have seen a great light. And for those who lived in the land where death casts its shadow, a light has shined. From then on Jesus began

to preach, 'Repent of your sins and turn to God, for the Kingdom of Heaven is near'" (Matthew 4:16).

What are the things that Jesus rewards?

"After all, what gives us hope and joy, and what will be our proud reward and crown as we stand before our Lord Jesus when he returns? It is you! Yes, you are our pride and joy" (1 Thessalonians 2:19).

Why does Jesus look for the lost?

"Christ suffered for our sins once for all time. He never sinned, but he died for sinners to bring you safely home to God" (1 Peter 3:18).

How do I know when to turn around and look for the lost?

If you have been lost, what was it like to be found?

How does looking for the one in the dark make me more like Jesus?

7

Looking For The One
WHO IS HUNGRY

*"It is Christ who pines when the poor are hungry; it is
Christ who is repulsed when strangers are not welcome;
it is Christ who suffers when rags fail to keep out the cold;
it is Christ who is in anguish in the long-drawn illness;
it is Christ who waits behind the prison doors."*

Archbishop William Temple (1628-1699)

THE MAN HOLDING THE SIGN is trying to make eye contact with me, but I refuse to look. After all, the light is about to turn green. Plus, I don't have any food, and if I give him money, it might end up in a bottle. As I drive past him, I see his handwritten sign. "Homeless. Anything helps."

Jesus has a beautiful way of addressing our hearts' issues. In my case, he spoke to me about hunger at a conference in Nashville for Christian radio stations. After a long day of meetings and concerts, there was a reception that included dessert. Around 10 PM, I headed for the exit and happened to walk past the kitchen. As I glanced inside, I saw trays covered with cookies.

If you have a soft spot for cookies, you know there is a considerable difference between the packaged cookies that are several weeks old and warm cookies emerging from an oven. These cookies were freshly made. They were enormous, and they were delicious.

Since one of our waiters was nearby, I asked, "What happens to all this?"

"Unfortunately, it goes to waste."

There was a moment of inspiration. "I have a question. Would you allow me to take some of these and give them away to people living on the streets?"

I loved his response. "Absolutely!"

Moments later, I walked through downtown Nashville looking for the one. But on this night, I found a community. A group of homeless men lived in various locations around Nashville and, at the moment, were seated on the steps of an old building. The street was dark, yet I felt safe as I approached with my bags of food.

The men on the steps were polite, but it was apparent as they began to eat: these men were hungry. I sat down on the steps, and their stories began to unfold. Stories of loss and regret. The pain of being so needy and dependent. As I walked back to the hotel, conviction set in with all the times I had chosen to look away. As I woke up during the night, I thought about this community of men sleeping somewhere on the streets.

I knew that I would look for opportunities to feed the hungry from that day on. Because of the men on the steps, I would look for opportunities to hear their stories.

On my next trip to Costco, I purchased several boxes of protein bars. I kept the bars in the front seat next to bottles of water and copies of the Salvation Poem. Instead of looking away, I was looking for my next "appointment."

One of my appointments was with a young man who stood on the same corner in downtown Minneapolis almost every day. I gave

Ronnie protein bars and bottles of water and shared with him about Jesus. I discovered that he had no family. He had no home. Then one day, Ronnie was standing on the corner wearing a dress and a pair of nylons. He spoke in a feminine voice as he thanked me for the food. A few days later, we had our first cold snap of the year. By cold snap, I mean wind chills well below zero. As I drove to work, I hoped and prayed that Ronnie would not be standing on that corner. But there he was in a dress and a pair of high heels. When Ronnie walked over to my car, he was shaking so severely that he could barely speak.

As I gave Ronnie the protein bars, I told him that there was no way he would spend the day in these conditions. Then I asked if I could take him to the Union Gospel Mission. I told him that I knew the staff and that he would be safe, warm, and welcome.

The moment Ronnie sensed my determination to help him, his face grew hard. Then his face contorted with anger. As he turned to walk away, he said, "No."

That was the last word that Ronnie spoke to me. He was no longer at his corner the next day, and I never saw him again.

I don't know what happened in Ronnie's life that caused him to walk away. I don't know what corner he might be standing on today. All I know is that Jesus loves Ronnie and is looking for him. Because Jesus loves Ronnie, he is sending someone to look for him.

If we believe that someone is beyond the reach of Jesus, we need to enjoy a few meals with Jesus. "But when the teachers of religious law who were Pharisees saw him eating with tax collectors and other sinners, they asked his disciples, 'Why does he eat with such scum?' When Jesus heard this, he told them, 'Healthy people don't need a doctor—sick people do. I have come to call not those who think they are righteous, but those who know they are sinners'" (Mark 2:16-17).

If we believe that the hungry don't matter, we don't understand our inheritance. "Then the King will say to those on his right, 'Come, you who are blessed by my Father, inherit the Kingdom prepared for you from the creation of the world. For I was hungry, and you fed me. I was thirsty, and you gave me a drink. I was a stranger, and you invited me into your home. I was naked, and you gave me clothing. I was sick, and you cared for me. I was in prison, and you visited me... I tell you the truth, when you did it to one of the least of these my brothers and sisters, you were doing it to me!'" (Matthew 25:34-40)

When a memorial service for George Floyd was held a block away from the PraiseLive Minneapolis studio, there was no hesitation from our team. We set up tents near the entrance and brought in cold bottles of water and protein bars. Because of Covid we gave away face masks and hand sanitizer. The banner on our tent was an invitation to be prayed for. In the hours before the service, we noticed a long row of media and saw logos from around the world. Then we noticed that many of them had no water. Our team went person to person and were honored to give a cup of cold water in the name of Jesus. One reporter from the Middle East opened up about his spiritual background and with questions about Jesus.

As the service was about to begin, we saw a group of people approaching, wearing matching blue shirts. It was the Billy Graham Rapid Response Team. They were delighted to share our tents and go with us through the crowds as we shared Jesus one by one.

A Somalian mother needed a place to nurse her baby, and our team created a safe place for her. An atheist stopped by and discovered that we were not there to debate her. We were there to serve her. We visited a group of homeless people living in tents. Near the end of the service, I noticed a large group of young men standing on a nearby soccer field. They were listening to the service from a distance, and now it was the most natural thing in the world to carry a basket of water bottles to them.

When it comes to loving one another, I know we have a long way to go. I know that it is overwhelming. But what if we were to begin by loving one person at a time? Recently, I was driving in downtown Minneapolis on a Sunday morning. As I saw the man standing on the corner with his sign, I reached for my protein bars. The van in front of me stopped, and a guy wearing a hard hat leaned out and handed the man a large paper bag. As I pulled up to the corner, he smiled and said, "Man, he just gave me his whole lunch."

Jesus spoke to thousands of people, but over and over, he took time for the one. He asks us to love the one. "And if you give even a cup of cold water to one of the least of my followers, you will surely be rewarded" (Matthew 10:42).

One smile. One bottle of water.

One whole lunch, so that one person sees the face of Jesus.

REFLECT:

When I see someone holding a sign, do I look away?

Is there a ministry where I can serve?

EQUIP:

How do I look for the one who is hungry?

MAKE A PLAN: One of the keys to meeting a need is making a plan. Pray about what you can give to ministries directly involved in meeting needs. Better yet, pray about how you can get involved in meeting a need. Changing the oil on a car, mowing a lawn, bringing meals, or babysitting are gifts with a personal touch.

MODEL COMPASSION: During a record cold snap, my friend Kyle and his family purchased several blankets. As they drove through Minneapolis, they wrapped several people in the love of Jesus. Kyle shared that now when his daughter sees someone standing in the cold, she asks, "Dad, do they need a blanket?"

DON'T FORGET: There are people who are hungry because we are forgetful. "And don't forget to do good and to share with those in need. These are the sacrifices that please God" (Hebrews 13:16).

LET'S PRAY:

Jesus, forgive me for all of the times I have looked away. Forgive me for not loving my brother or my sister. Instead of being overwhelmed and discouraged, I look to you to show me the one. I reach out in your precious name and ask that as my hand touches a place of need, there is a revelation of you.

DISCUSS:

Have you ever struggled to find food? Did someone help you?

How does Jesus respond to hunger?

"Then Jesus called his disciples and told them, 'I feel sorry for these people. They have been here with me for three days, and they have nothing left to eat. I don't want to send them away hungry, or they will faint along the way'" (Matthew 15:32).

Why does Paul share that he has been hungry?

"I have worked hard and long, enduring many sleepless nights. I have been hungry and thirsty and have often gone without food. I have shivered in the cold, without enough clothing to keep me warm" (2 Corinthians 11:27).

How does caring for people purify us?

"Pure and genuine religion in the sight of God the Father means caring for orphans and widows in their distress and refusing to let the world corrupt you" (James 1:27).

How does caring for the hungry bless us?

"Feed the hungry, and help those in trouble. Then your light will shine out from the darkness, and the darkness around you will be as bright as noon" (Isaiah 58:10).

How do we "Love your neighbor as yourself?" (Mark 12:31)
What is our future hope?

"They will never again be hungry or thirsty; they will never be scorched by the heat of the sun. For the Lamb on the throne will be their Shepherd. He will lead them to springs of life-giving water. And God will wipe every tear from their eyes" (Revelation 7:16-17).

As I look for the one who is hungry, how am I becoming more like Jesus?

8

Looking For The One
WHO NEEDS TO PLAY CATCH

*"For this is what the Sovereign Lord says: I myself will search
and find my sheep. I will be like a shepherd looking for his
scattered flock. I will find my sheep and rescue them from all the
places where they were scattered on that dark and cloudy day."*

Ezekiel 34:11-12

"HOW DO YOU KNOW who is the one?" I looked up at Aaron and saw the question in his eyes. He wanted to know. When Aaron walks into a room, people notice. As a pitcher in major league baseball and a man who stands 6' 9", Aaron Slegers gets your attention. But what I respect about Aaron is that his attention is on you when he walks into the room. I remember years ago hearing that there are two kinds of people. People who walk into the room and announce, "Here I am." And the people who walk into the room and say, "There you are!"

As Aaron and I sat in my rental car outside of a pizza place in Fort Myers, we were talking about looking for the one. Now Aaron asked the million-dollar question: "How do you know who is the one?" Before walking into the restaurant, we took a moment to ask Jesus to show us the one. We prayed, "Jesus, please make it so clear that we can't miss it!"

As we waited for the waitress to arrive, I slowly looked around the room. Was there an appointment with someone looking for Jesus? We talked about strategy for a moment, and then I had an idea. "Aaron, let's toss the ball to our waitress a few times and see if she wants to play catch."

When our waitress arrived, she was in a hurry and quickly dropped off our menu. I looked around to see if someone sitting near us might be open to a conversation. No one stood out, and no one looked in our direction. When our waitress returned to take our order, I noticed the weariness on her face and wondered if she was in pain. I breathed a prayer, "Holy Spirit, what question would unlock her heart?"

As I looked into her eyes, a question came to me. "I sense that there is a story of how you came to Fort Myers. What brought you here?" She hesitated and then quietly said, "I lived for years in an abusive marriage. I tried over and over to leave. Last year I finally got up the courage to start over. I wish I had done it years ago, but that is what brought me to Fort Myers."

When you look for the one, you find yourself in two conversations at once—the conversation with the person and the conversation with the Holy Spirit. As I listened and prayed, I felt prompted to say, "As Aaron and I pray for our meal, we will pray for you. You heard so many painful and untrue things during those years of abuse. We are going to pray that lies are replaced with truth." Because the restaurant was starting to fill up, she thanked us and hurried to the next table.

The pizza was delicious, and when it was time to pay our bill, she was nowhere in sight. Once again, the whisper of the Holy Spirit: "Go and look for her." As Aaron and I arrived at the back of the restaurant, she was walking out of the break room. She smiled, "I just finished my break. Thanks again for coming in."

If you ever doubt the providence of God, go looking for the one. You have a front-row seat to the God who orders your steps because He is looking for the one. He timed our arrival before the rush of customers. He timed her break to end as we were about to leave. He oversaw the kitchen staff so that we were not interrupted. So I asked a question.

"I have a friend that wrote a short poem that explains how you can begin a relationship with Jesus. Can I share the Salvation Poem with you?" She smiled, "I've just been thinking about going back to church. I would like that."

On most days, I carry a copy of The Salvation Poem, and I read these words to her:

> Jesus, you died upon a cross
> And rose again to save the lost
> Forgive me now of all my sin
> Come be my Savior, Lord, and Friend
> Change my life and make it new
> And help me, Lord, to live for you

For several years I would read the poem and then ask if they believed that Jesus died on the cross. There is a better question. "Do you know why Jesus died on the cross?" In Brennan McPherson's book, *The Simple Gospel*, he shares some of the reasons:

> God is holy, and our sin separates us from him (Romans 3:23).
>
> Jesus was beaten for our sins, and his punishment brings us peace and healing (Isaiah 53:1-12).
>
> Our debt to God was nailed to the cross, satisfying God's justness (1 John 2:2).

> Christ took our curse by being hung on a tree to free us from the curse of sin (Galatians 3:13-14).

> In essence, Jesus died to bring us to God (John 12:32).

As Brennan summarizes, "He tasted death for us so that we could taste life."

In essence, if someone does not understand the bad news, you will find that they are not ready to receive the good news. It was clear that our waitress understood the bad news of sin that separates us from God and results in broken relationships. She understood why Jesus had died on the cross for her. When I asked if she could remember when she had prayed, "Forgive me now of all my sin," she could not remember praying something like that.

Now it was time for the good news. "If you confess your sins to Jesus and invite him into your life, he offers to be your Savior, Lord, and Friend. *Savior* means a brand-new start as you are forgiven and adopted by Jesus. *Lord* means that you are no longer in charge of your life and surrender to Jesus. *Friend* means that you now have a friend that will never leave you or forsake you."

I asked her, "Would you like Jesus to be your Savior, Lord, and Friend?" Her eyes filled with joy as she said, "Yes!" I led her through a prayer of repentance, and she invited Jesus to be her Savior, Lord, and Friend.

As she said amen and raised her head, a voice behind us spoke. "I've been praying for this day!" We turned and saw a young waitress. Her eyes were alive with joy as she threw her arms around her and said, "Mom, I'm so happy for you!"

Jesus had ordered a daughter's steps to witness her mother's prayer and be the first to welcome her home. How great is our God!

Aaron turned to me as we walked back to our car, "So do you think she was the one?!"

REFLECT:

When I walk into a room, am I looking for the one?

EQUIP:

How do I look for the one who needs to play catch?

EYES TO SEE: Be encouraged that Jesus has already gone ahead of you as you look for the one. He is softening hearts and ordering steps on your behalf. As you look for the one, pray that you have eyes to see and the wisdom to know what questions to ask. "I pray that the eyes of your heart may be enlightened in order that you may know the hope to which he has called you, the riches of his glorious inheritance in his holy people" (Ephesians 1:18).

ALL HAVE SINNED: Our family was waiting in the lobby of a movie theater, and I noticed a woman vacuuming up the popcorn from the carpet. As I began to share the gospel I shared that "all have sinned" from Romans 3:23. She held her hand up and then looked at me with a straight face. "My sister has sinned but I have never sinned." In her case there was no open door for the gospel until there was conviction of sin.

MAKE THE FIRST THROW: As you initiate conversations and look for common ground, you invite someone to stand with you at the foot of the cross. Questions from the heart can open a heart. As someone responds to you, God prepares their heart to respond to him. Sometimes a first question is the only question you need to ask! "When Jesus saw him and knew he had been ill for a long time, he asked him, 'Would you like to get well?'" (John 5:6)

LET'S PRAY:

Jesus, I surrender my steps to you. Direct my life into the path of someone who needs to know you. As I look into their eyes, help me see through your eyes. Please show me the right questions to ask. Give me boldness to present the Gospel and the price you paid because of our sins with clarity. Jesus, only you can open their eyes, and I pray that you would open my eyes as I look for the one.

DISCUSS:

Why did Jesus die on the cross?

"He personally carried our sins in his body on the cross so that we can be dead to sin and live for what is right. By his wounds you are healed. Once you were like sheep who wandered away. But now you have turned to your Shepherd, the Guardian of your souls" (1 Peter 2:24-25).

Is "playing catch" in a conversation hard for you? What are some questions that invite someone to open up?

How does someone serving you see the light of Jesus?

"You are the light of the world—like a city on a hilltop that cannot be hidden. No one lights a lamp and then puts it under a basket. Instead, a lamp is placed on a stand, where it gives light to everyone in the house. In the same way, let your good deeds shine out for all to see, so that everyone will praise your heavenly Father" (Matthew 5:14-16).

When you go to other towns, does the gospel travel with you?

"But Jesus replied, 'We must go on to other towns as well, and I will preach to them, too. That is why I came'" (Mark 1:38).

As I play catch with someone who is lost, how do I become more like Jesus?

9

Looking For The One
WHO IS A SPARROW WATCHER

"He is the God of details. He knows the name of every star, He counts every hair by number, He pays attention to every sparrow, He clothes the flowers with splendor, and His thoughts toward you cannot be numbered."

Roy Lessin

AS I WALKED INTO Whole Foods Market in downtown Minneapolis, I prayed, "Lord, show me the one." As I made my way through the produce and frozen foods, I began to look. As I approached the cashiers, there was no indicator who was on God's heart. At this particular Whole Foods, the windows overlook Washington Avenue. It's a busy street with a view of the Minneapolis skyline. I stood for a moment watching the pedestrians and traffic bustle down the street.

Suddenly there was a "thump" against the window. I looked and saw a sparrow lying on the ground. At first, it was motionless, and then its wings fluttered ever so slightly. Then a woman standing next to me quietly said, "Oh my God."

People around us refer to God even if they don't know him. Sometimes it is profanity, but sometimes it is an invitation for a relationship. As I turned, I saw a woman's face filled with compassion.

Her next words surprised me. "I'm going outside to check on the bird."

There was little doubt about who I was looking for by this time, so I followed her outside. Over the sounds of the traffic, I heard her say, "You're okay. You're going to make it." She knelt down and cradled the bird. Then she gently began to stroke the head of the sparrow.

The next several minutes were surreal. To my left, traffic was bustling by, and to my right, a lady was whispering to a sparrow. Within moments, she was on the phone with a nature center and informed by a staff member that birds can be dazed for 15-20 minutes before recovering. If there is no recovery in that time frame, you have a bird that will not make it.

I use task management software that is very helpful in scheduling the priorities for each day. You can give each item deadlines and priority codes. I've noticed that I frequently find the one who needs Jesus when I am overwhelmed. I've also noticed that he always makes up for the "lost" time. The person is not on my "to do" list, but they are on God's heart.

When I am tempted not to take time for people, I think about my friend Vern Anderson. For many years Vern was the CEO of Douglas Machine in Alexandria. During the early days of the Promise Keepers movement, I invited Vern to join an accountability group. Four of us met almost every Friday for over ten years, but one of the first meetings was the most memorable. Vern shared that Douglas was facing a financial shortfall and that, barring millions of dollars in orders, they would have to begin laying off employees. We prayed for 15 minutes, and then we prayed for an hour. Then we prayed until we lost track of time. All at once, everyone in the room knew that we had broken through.

Vern called at noon to share that orders were coming in from around the world. We prayed again and asked Jesus to finish what

He had started. More orders came in that afternoon, and there were millions of dollars in revenue by that evening. It was the largest day for orders in the company's history.

As I spent time with Vern, I saw the pattern. Vern took time to pray and prioritized time for people.

I let go of my "to do" list as I thought of Vern. I relaxed and began to ask questions and listen for this sparrow watcher's heart. Her life was filled with traveling and activity in social and political movements. As she held the sparrow, she spoke of a life of compassion.

As I listened, I prayed for her, and I prayed for the sparrow in her hands. I finally asked if I could share something that Jesus said during his time on earth. She nodded her approval, and I began to read from the YouVersion app: "What is the price of two sparrows—one copper coin? But not a single sparrow can fall to the ground without your Father knowing it. And the very hairs on your head are all numbered. So don't be afraid; you are more valuable to God than a whole flock of sparrows" (Matthew 10:29-30).

I told her that people have believed that God is distant or disapproving for centuries. But when Jesus came to earth, he shared that he cares about the sparrows and cares for us. He came to seek and save us. God loved us so much that he sent his son Jesus to die on the cross for our sins.

As I looked into her eyes, I said, "I don't believe the sparrow crashing into that window was random or an accident. I think it happened so that you would know the God who watches sparrows and who numbers the hairs on your head. He loves you and wants you to know him. I believe that the compassion you have is a gift from him." As I shared the Salvation Poem with her, I watched her face.

Some people hear about Jesus, and it's like watching a flower turn toward the sun. They open up and come to life before your eyes. This woman began to open up and come to life. She started to ask questions, and then a cloud came over her face. Something stood in her way. A memory or a fear, but as quickly as she opened up, her eyes darkened. She dropped her head and withdrew from the conversation.

My heart broke as I saw her sitting at the table, holding a lifeless bird.

I don't know why some people experience the love of Jesus and run away. Why do some people spend a lifetime refusing his love? All I know is that we are called to share the love of Jesus and pray that he opens hearts to the gospel.

As I turned to leave, her face lit up. The sparrow was coming to life.

REFLECT:

Am I willing to set aside time for people?

Am I willing to hear a curse so that I can speak a blessing?

EQUIP:

How do I look for a sparrow watcher?

CARE FOR SPARROWS: As a young boy, I recall the day a baby bird fell from its nest into our yard. As one of the cats on our farm quickly moved forward, a tall figure stepped in the way and scooped up the bird. Then he found an extension ladder and restored the bird to its nest. The rescuer that day was my Uncle Hudson Armerding. At the time Hudson was serving as the president of Wheaton College. On this day

I understood one of the reasons he was given the responsibility of caring for college students. Hudson cared for sparrows.

SURRENDER YOUR TIME: As you plan your day, dare to believe that God can make up the unexpected time you invest in people. You are choosing to love what he loves. As you pray, dare to believe that God can do more than you can ask or think.

HEAR THEIR CRY: Sometimes you hear, "Oh my God." Other times the name of Jesus is hurled as a curse. You will find that the one cursing God frequently tries to push you away. The curse is a cry for help.

LET'S PRAY:

Jesus, I can relate to someone you loved named Martha. I am worried and upset over all these details. But today, I surrender my details to you. I know that I can trust you because you love me. You number the hairs on my head. I am willing to surrender my schedule to reach one sparrow watcher.

DISCUSS:

How is God revealed in creation?

"For ever since the world was created, people have seen the earth and sky. Through everything God made, they can clearly see his invisible qualities—his eternal power

and divine nature. So they have no excuse for not knowing God" (Romans 1:20).

Why would God care about a helpless sparrow?

"When we were utterly helpless, Christ came at just the right time and died for us sinners" (Romans 5:6).

How do we respond when there is no response to the gospel?

"Do not despise these small beginnings, for the Lord rejoices to see the work begin..." (Zechariah 4:10).

How do you tend to respond to the one who is cursing?

How can you tell if a curse is a cry for help?

As I look for a sparrow watcher, how do I become more like Jesus?

10

Looking For The One
WHO NEEDS TO FORGIVE

"Forgiveness is setting a prisoner free and then
discovering the prisoner was you."

John Eldredge

"YOU NEED TO FORGIVE HIM before you reach the interstate." The conviction was unmistakable. It was the prompting of the Holy Spirit.

I had been thinking about forgiving someone for several months. As I drove north toward the interstate, it consumed my thoughts. But on this day, the Spirit of God drew a line across the highway. My disobedience needed to be settled once and for all. As the miles went by, I thought about the offense. I replayed the conversation and the things spoken against me. Now the pressure intensified as I saw the bridge over the interstate approaching.

Moments before reaching the bridge, I finally chose to forgive. It was a brief prayer that felt like tearing a bandage off a wound. There was a searing moment of pain but then instant relief. As I confessed my sin of unforgiveness, I was at complete peace and not distracted for the first time in weeks.

Halfway across the bridge, a car pulled out in front of me.

I hit the brakes and threw the steering wheel to the left. I experienced the remarkable sensation of sliding down the road sideways. The sound of squealing tires was piercing. As I came to a shuddering halt, I looked to my right. The other car was inches from my vehicle. An older man was in the fetal position, his head pressed against his hands.

He slowly raised his gaze and saw my smiling face. I waved and drove away, knowing what had saved both of us. It was forgiveness. If I had crossed the interstate as a distracted driver, there was no way I would have reacted in time.

Jesus made it crystal clear that forgiveness is not optional. "If you forgive those who sin against you, your heavenly Father will forgive you. But if you refuse to forgive others, your Father will not forgive your sins" (Matthew 6:14-15).

As a college student, I worked for two summers at a Bible camp in northern Minnesota. During a junior-high camp, two teenage boys got into several fights. I finally met with one of the guys and handed him a baseball bat. I asked him to squeeze the bat for as long and as hard as possible. As his friends gathered around, he decided it was a perfect opportunity to show off his upper body strength. As he gripped the bat, he began to glisten with sweat. Then as he held the bat, he quickly became exhausted. When he finally let go, he could barely open his hands. It was time to speak a word to him.

"Your fighting and your unforgiveness are like holding this bat. It feels good. It feels powerful. But anger and unforgiveness are going to wear you out. It is going to exhaust you." He said nothing, but the two boys never fought again.

Unforgiveness distracts us and wears us out, but it also divides us.

I was seated at my desk on a beautiful summer day in our downtown Minneapolis studio. One of the staff whispered, "We have a situation." From the look on our receptionist's face, I knew it was serious. As I came down the hallway, I could hear the voice of a young woman demanding access to our studio. She had a message for our audience. She needed to go on air right now.

As I came around the corner, I saw a young lady who had dyed her afro bright red and green. Suddenly, building security appeared, and she locked her eyes on me. I tried to calm her, but her voice became louder and louder.

Her words broke the silence. "I see what's going on." She turned and disappeared into the streets of downtown Minneapolis.

For some reason, the encounter with this young lady bothered me. I could not escape the look on her face as she turned to leave. I wondered what it was she wanted to share on the air. One day I asked Jesus to help me find her.

Several months later, the impossible happened. I had just finished lunch at a downtown restaurant, and as I got up to leave, I saw a familiar face seated in the corner. The still small voice of the Holy Spirit was immediate. "You need to ask for forgiveness." As I walked up to her table, he whispered again, "You need to kneel."

As I knelt beside her table, I quietly said: "I don't know if you remember me…"

As she looked away, I heard a whisper, "I remember you."

"I have thought many times about the day you stopped by. I've wanted to ask your forgiveness for how we treated you so many times. I hope you can forgive me."

Now she turns to look into my eyes. "I forgive you."

It turns out that this beautiful young lady works at a grocery store in downtown Minneapolis. Whenever possible, I purchase groceries in her store and get into her checkout line. She laughs at my attempts to buy healthy food, and I look into her eyes and ask how she is doing.

Because of Jesus, she is my friend.

Imagine the scene when Jesus was washing the feet of his disciples. The Son of God wrapping himself in a towel and kneeling before people like you and me. Listen to the prayer of Jesus, "I pray that they will all be one" (John 17:21).

Because of Jesus, we kneel together in prayer.

Because of Jesus, we kneel to ask forgiveness.

You are probably thinking of at least one relationship that needs reconciliation. Ask Jesus to show you the posture to take as you approach this person. Is it a phone call, a handwritten note, or kneeling beside them? As you spend time with Jesus, ask him to give you a glimpse of their heart. Before reaching out, ask Jesus to bless this person. You will watch in wonder as Jesus softens your heart. "But I say, love your enemies! Pray for those who persecute you" (Matthew 5:44).

You may have someone who has refused to forgive you. Years ago, I asked for forgiveness and instead was the recipient of months of gossip. In my distress, our son Jordan made an observation. "Dad, you pray so many times that you would decrease, and Jesus would increase. Is it possible that he is allowing this to answer your prayer?" Two things happened after that observation. I was at peace, and the gossip ceased.

I first heard the Holy Spirit's voice as a first grader on a school bus. For several weeks the older kids in the back of the bus had been pelting me with corn and making fun of my jacket. (I fed the pigs each morning and later discovered that my jacket reeked of pig manure.) I heard an audible voice as I sat there fighting back the tears. "Forgive them, for they don't know what they are doing" (Luke 23:34). I was unaware that these were the words of Jesus on the cross until hearing this passage shared in a sermon.

As you struggle to forgive, remember the cross of Christ.

REFLECT:

Who do I need to forgive?

Who needs to forgive me?

EQUIP:

How do I look for the one who needs to forgive?

BEGIN WITH JESUS: Have you approached Jesus for his forgiveness? So many times, we make the people around us the focus of forgiveness. But David lifts a profound prayer in the Psalms. "Feel my pain and see my trouble. Forgive all my sins" (Psalm 25:18).

PRAY A BLESSING: Decades ago I discovered something powerful. As I forgave someone who had repeatedly wounded me, there seemed to be a barrier. I was still wounded and offended. When I considered the challenge of Jesus to love your enemies and pray for those who persecute you, I began to pray a blessing. If you were to listen in the first few days you would discern the halfhearted nature of these prayers. But several weeks later I was crying out for God to bless this one and show his favor to them. Halfhearted forgiveness only heals half of your heart.

FIND THE PATH: As you kneel in prayer, ask Jesus to show you the path to reconciliation. Ask him for the posture to adopt in drawing near. "The Lord is good and does what is right; he shows the proper path to those who go astray" (Psalm 25:8).

LET'S PRAY:

Jesus, thank you for forgiving me. I was lost and deserving wrath, but you gave your life for me. In light of your sacrifice on the cross, I choose to forgive. You are the righteous judge, and I turn this person over to you. Forgive them, for they do not know what they are doing. Now guide me on how to be reconciled with my brother and my sister. Please show me the posture to adopt in approaching them. Thank you for lifting the distraction of disobedience and releasing the joy of obedience!

DISCUSS:

What does it mean to "make allowance"?

"Make allowance for each other's faults, and forgive anyone who offends you. Remember, the Lord forgave you, so you must forgive others" (Colossians 3:13).

Who is most challenging for you to forgive?

If you forgive someone, do you feel like you are letting them off the hook?

"For we know the one who said, 'I will take revenge. I will pay them back'" (Hebrews 10:30).

What kind of offense takes the longest to get over?

Are you willing to forgive yourself and forget the failures of the past?

> *"When God forgives and restores his people, he wants them to forget the failures of the past, witness for him in the present, and claim his promises for the future. Why should we remember that which God has forgotten?"* (Warren Wiersbe)

As I look for the one who needs to forgive me, how do I become more like Jesus?

11

Looking For The One
ON YOUR FLIGHT

*"You see me when I travel and when I rest at
home. You know everything I do."*

Psalm 139:3

I AM BOOKING a flight, and as I look at the available seats, I ask the Holy Spirit to show me his seat assignment. There are the aisle seats near the front that I want and seats in the back by the restroom that are less desirable. But my heart is to select the seat assigned to me by the Lord. Someone on this flight needs Jesus, and my heart is to sit next to them. Someone on this flight is my guest of honor.

Suddenly, I feel drawn to a particular location.

As an ambassador for Christ, you can watch a movie, read a book, or look for the one when you travel on a flight. On a trip to Nashville, I sat next to an atheist, and he shared his views on the Church and God's existence. He was confident and very loud. I could feel my face turning red as people around us leaned in to listen to our conversation.

When you find yourself in a moment like this, you have the option of engaging in a debate. A stranger punches, and you counterpunch. It's probably my lack of skill as a debater, but I have rarely found that helpful. It works for me to change the subject and ask

Jesus to show me their heart. I ask about their work, then about their family, and then about their hopes and dreams.

Ask questions, listen, and pray.

On this flight, my guest of honor began to lower his voice and then opened up about a spiritual leader who had abused a family member. There was finally an opportunity to share the hope of Jesus and even the plan of salvation. My new friend listened intently, but as the flight landed, he was not interested in a relationship with Christ.

Can I encourage you not to put your hope in what you can see in these moments? No matter the response, God's Word never returns void. As Lee Strobel once observed, "You will never regret being courageous for Christ."

As I stood up to retrieve my bag from the overhead compartment, a man behind me asked if he could have a word.

"My wife is dying, and I am flying home to spend my last days with her. Thank you. I needed to hear that." This man didn't need to hear an argument in the midst of such pain. He didn't need my debate skills or pride. What he needed was gentle good news.

On a flight from London to Minneapolis, the middle-aged man next to me was agitated. Then he started making trips to the restroom every ten or fifteen minutes. I noticed beads of sweat on Mike's face and asked if he was okay. Mike explained, "When I fly, I get panic attacks." Over the next several hours, we talked about his life in Europe and the overwhelming pressure he faced as an engineer. He shared his desire to someday be married. I walked Mike through the Salvation Poem, and as we began our descent, I prayed a blessing over Mike.

A few days later, Mike emailed from Europe and shared that he was still thinking about our conversation and had begun to listen to PraiseLive on his computer. Mike would tell me when he was listening, and I dedicated songs and verses to him. I led our listening family in praying over his life. As Mike turned to Jesus, he turned away from depression and suicidal thoughts.

When you step onto an airplane looking for the one, it changes how you see the people around you. You can't wait to help an older woman with her bag or help to cheer up the children who are crying across the aisle. Looking for the one changes how you ask, "Are you okay?" People sense the mercy and compassion of Jesus.

On a flight from Minneapolis to London, we gathered at the gate for the boarding process. As the first-class passengers began to move forward, a woman cried out, "I've lost my passport." She was frantic. As several people gathered around, she explained that she had placed her passport on her tray while eating lunch. She pointed to a large garbage can that was overflowing. "My passport is in that garbage can."

I've worked my share of dirty jobs. At a Bible camp, I cleaned restrooms for two summers. At Bethel University, I scraped and rinsed thousands of cafeteria trays. Of course, none of that compared to growing up on a dairy farm with 52 cows. As Dad used to say, "No manure, no milk."

There was no time to find a pair of gloves or call for help, so I found an empty garbage can just around the corner. I took a deep breath and began moving items from the full can to the empty can. By this time, a crowd has gathered to watch the festivities. When I lifted out something extra juicy, they oohed and aahed. When I found her tray with the leftover salad, they saw her excitement turn to disappointment. Finally, the entire garbage can was empty. No passport.

Now the boarding area was nearly empty, and as she was fighting back the tears, I asked if we could take a moment to pray.

Some of the most powerful prayers in the Bible are only a few words. Deep theological prayers like, "Lord, save us!" (Matthew 8:25) Or one of my mom's favorite prayers, "Lord, have mercy..." (Psalm 41:10).

This prayer was only a few words: "Jesus, help us find the passport."

I can't explain it, but during that brief prayer, Jesus showed me where her passport was. I don't know how to explain it, but I just knew. It's like when you know that blue is your favorite color or that you are supposed to call a friend and check in on them. We know because Jesus said, "My sheep listen to my voice" (John 10:27).

I gently told the woman, "Your passport is in your purse."

She blurted out, "That's impossible! It was on my tray, and I checked my purse. I've checked every pocket in this purse."

As the flight crew stared at us, I heard myself say, "You need to check again because your passport is in your purse."

As she began to empty her purse, I saw her eyes drawn to a small zippered compartment. She unzipped it, reached inside, and pulled out her passport! There was no time to celebrate or wash my hands, so we hurried down the ramp to get on the plane.

Several people recognized her when she walked into the plane and they began to cheer. Then something extraordinary happened. As she walked down the aisle, she waved her passport above her head and announced over and over, "We prayed! We prayed!"

Sometimes I close my eyes and try to imagine what God is doing in a moment like that. A passport is lost because someone has given up on prayer or walked away from their faith. Or someone who thinks that Christians are judgmental or distant is watching the garbage can.

Then I think of the woman who lost her passport. One moment she is frantic and has no hope.

Now she lifts off for London, knowing that Jesus is real.

REFLECT:

Are there times when I know that Jesus is speaking to me?

What is something he is speaking about today?

EQUIP:

How do I look for the one on my flight?

PRAYER ASSIGNMENT: On your next flight, pray over your seat assignment. Even if an airline computer chooses your seat, pray over the divine appointment that God may have in the seat next to you. Be alert to a mom with young children or an older person trying to stow their bag in the overhead bin. If your assignment is someone who wishes to argue about Christianity, change the subject to Jesus. Ask questions, listen, and pray.

QUESTIONS THAT OPEN DOORS: Look for open-ended questions as conversation starters:

Are you headed home?

What do you love the most about your work?

Do you have a family?

By the way, if your assignment involves a lost passport, pray before you begin digging through the garbage. Just a thought!

LET'S PRAY:

Jesus, someone has been running from you, and because you love them, they are seated next to me. On my own, I have no chance of unraveling the mystery of their heart. But you are the revealer of secrets, and you can open my eyes to their hidden pain and questions. I am available because, "Where can they go from your Spirit?" (Psalm 139:7)

DISCUSS:

Why do you guide a conversation toward Jesus?

"And this is the way to have eternal life—to know you, the only true God, and Jesus Christ, the one you sent to earth" (John 17:3).

How do you guide a conversation to the person of Jesus?

"There is salvation in no one else! God has given no other name under heaven by which we must be saved" (Acts 4:12).

What is a story that you can tell a stranger about Jesus?

"We cannot stop telling about everything we have seen and heard" (Acts 4:20).

What are some great questions to ask a stranger?

How do you change a debate into a conversation?

How do I become more like Jesus as I look for the one on my flight?

12

Looking For The One
WHO NEEDS TO DELIGHT

"Let us therefore desire nothing else, wish for nothing else, and let nothing please and delight us except our Creator and Redeemer, and Savior, the only true God."

Francis of Assisi

AS THE CHAPEL SERVICE ended, one guy stayed behind. As he hung his head, he quietly said, "I'm having trouble with my computer." From years of men's Bible studies and chapels, I have learned that men often speak in code.

"By trouble with my computer, do you mean you are spending time on the wrong kind of websites?"

"Yes."

What tumbled out was the story of a man who loves Jesus and has battled pornography for decades. He described discovering porn as a teenager and the slow progression to addiction. My heart ached as he shared the impact of this one sin issue on his walk with Jesus. He told me that his wife did not know, but his marriage would be over if she ever found out. I asked questions and listened to his heart, and then the Holy Spirit whispered a question.

"Is your Christian life all about sin management?" His eyes were puzzled. "In other words, do you think about this sin more than you think about Jesus?" He softly replied, "It's all I can think about. Even when I've been clean for a few weeks, I think about it every day."

"I have an assignment for you. Starting today, you are no longer in sin management. In other words, this sin is no longer the center of your Christian life. Starting today, I want you to delight in the Lord."

One of the first persons I observed delighting in the Lord was my Grandpa Armerding. Papa was a professor at Dallas Theological Seminary, and his students like Chuck Swindoll have spoken of his impact. He taught theology at Wheaton College and served with the Moody Bible Institute. He was known for the depth of his teaching. But when Papa came to visit, I loved to hear him preach because his face would become radiant. It wasn't an expression on his face. It was the love of Jesus expressed through his face.

During Papa's visits to our farm, I would sleep on the couch so he would have a private room. I walked past my bedroom one early morning and noticed the door was ajar. I tiptoed up to peek inside, and there he was, dressed in his suit and tie. He was holding God's Word, and his face was radiant.

At Papa's 90th birthday party, I discovered why his face was radiant. On a large sheet cake were the words to Papa's life verse: "One thing have I desired of the Lord, that will I seek after; that I may dwell in the house of the Lord all the days of my life, to behold the beauty of the Lord, and to inquire in his temple" (Psalm 27:4, KJV).

Papa lived for one thing. Because of Papa's delight in the Lord, I began to delight in the Lord. Now the mission statement for our radio ministry is part of his legacy: "Together we help people discover and worship Jesus."

Back in the stadium, there was a long pause and then a weighty question. "What do you mean by delight?" "This means that you love Jesus more than anything. Delight is our heart pressed against his heart, and instead of trying to earn his love, you receive his love. We don't have to hide when we stumble and fall." This one principle is life-changing: "Take delight in the Lord, and he will give you your heart's desire" (Psalm 37:4).

We talked for a few minutes about hidden sin that is like mold growing in the dark and the importance of stepping into the light and refusing to fight this battle alone. We discussed discipline and accountability. But then we returned to delight as I said, " If we lose our delight, we have no chance against sin."

I took a deep breath. "Now, this last thing is going to seem like the hardest thing. You'll be tempted to skip this step because it's too embarrassing. Instead of just confessing the sin of pornography, I want you to talk to your Abba Father about pornography. I want you to ask him why it has such a hold on your heart and you feel so hopeless. Take a notebook and when he starts to speak, start writing."

He shook his head, "I could never talk to him about that."

"Then you don't understand what it means to be adopted by him." According to Romans 8, we are adopted when we confess our sins and accept Jesus as Savior. "So you have not received a spirit that makes you fearful slaves. Instead, you received God's Spirit when he adopted you as his own children. Now we call him, 'Abba, Father'" (Romans 8:15).

We talked about the God who adopts us and then sings over his children. "For the Lord your God is living among you. He is a mighty savior. He will take delight in you with gladness. With his love, he will calm all your fears. He will rejoice over you with joyful songs" (Zephaniah 3:17).

As we walked out of the family room of the stadium, I thought of one more thing. "Sometime later today, you are going to regret this conversation. The thought will go through your mind that I think less of you. The truth is, I think more of you. Any regret or accusation is from satan. He wants to keep you alone and in the dark. You have just taken the first step into the light."

In the weeks that followed, I thought many times about the conversation in the stadium. As a major league baseball player, I knew temptations surrounded him. It was life on the road. How could he possibly win the fight? A few weeks later, his team happened to come through the Twin Cities again. As I entered the visitor's locker room, I saw him standing at the other end of the room. He looked up and headed in my direction.

We met in the middle, and he wrapped me in his arms. As he lifted me into the air, he whispered, "It worked! It worked! I'm free!"

As we said goodbye, it took my breath away.

His face was radiant.

REFLECT:

How would you finish the sentence, "I'm having trouble with..."?

Is there a hidden sin that needs to be brought into the light?

Is your walk with Jesus sin management?

EQUIP:

How do I look for the one who needs to delight?

GOD'S AFFECTION FOR YOU: To prepare your heart in looking for the one who needs to delight, this beautiful description of God's heart is from Dane Ortlund: "Our sins darken our feelings of his gracious heart, but his heart cannot be diminished for his own people due to their sins any more than the sun's existence can be threatened due to the passing of a few wispy clouds or an extended thunderstorm. The sun is shining. It cannot stop. Clouds, no clouds—sin, no sin—the tender heart of the Son of God is shining on me. This is an unflappable affection". (*Gentle and Lowly*). Finding the one who needs to delight is being found by the one who delights in you. Your acceptance of God's tender heart equips you to share his tender heart.

DELIGHT IN GOD: If pornography is your battle, do not lose hope. As John Piper shared in a radio interview, "You can delight in God so deeply that the compulsive power of pornography loses its triumph in your life". Remember, "He gave his life to free us from every kind of sin, to cleanse us, and to make us his very own people, totally committed to doing good deeds" (Titus 2:14).

UNHURRIED TIME: A disciplined quiet time is vital to the Christian faith. But our times with Jesus are more than checking off a daily reading list or working our way through a list of prayer requests. We need times with Jesus that are unhurried and uninterrupted. Long walks at sunset as we lift the simplest song to him. Prayer times with no list of requests and no agenda other than his presence.

LISTEN FOR THE SONG: If raising your family is slowly draining you of delight, take a moment to be still. Remember the first time your eyes saw their eyes. Remember the first words and the first steps. If your children are young, gaze in wonder as they fall asleep. As you listen for their breath, listen for the sound of the God who sings over you. "For the Lord your God is living among you. He is a mighty savior. He will take delight in you with gladness. With his love, he will calm all your fears. He will rejoice over you with joyful songs" (Zephaniah 3:17).

GUARD YOUR HEART: If the pressure of work or ministry is slowly crushing your delight, join me in praying along with Roy Lessin: "Let us guard our hearts and keep our work for the Lord from becoming more consuming than our delight in the Lord." Finally, I have one favor to ask of you. As you move from duty to delight, please take notes.

Someday your story will set someone free.

LET'S PRAY:

Jesus, the sin that I am holding on to is an idol. Forgive me for idolatry and reducing my relationship with you to sin management. As I delight in you, I ask that my face will become radiant. Now clear my heart of any critical spirit that would hinder someone from daring to confess their sins to me. Please give me the wisdom to know what questions to ask and verses to share. As I make my way through this day, show me just one to bring into the light.

DISCUSS:

What are some of the reasons that we hide our sin?

"When the cool evening breezes were blowing, the man and his wife heard the Lord God walking about in the garden. So they hid from the Lord God among the trees" (Genesis 3:8).

Is there something controlling you?

"For you are a slave to whatever controls you" (2 Peter 2:19).

What can take God's place in your heart?

"Dear children, keep away from anything that might take God's place in your hearts" (1 John 5:21).

How is living a godly life possible?

"By his divine power, God has given us everything we need for living a godly life. We have received all of this by coming to know him, the one who called us to himself by means of his marvelous glory and excellence" (2 Peter 1:3).

How does holiness "happen"?

"Now may the God of peace make you holy in every way, and may your whole spirit and soul and body be kept

blameless until our Lord Jesus Christ comes again. God will make this happen, for he who calls you is faithful" (1 Thessalonians 5:23, 24).

How does delight banish evil?

"Let the wicked change their ways and banish the very thought of doing wrong. Let them turn to the Lord that he may have mercy on them. Yes, turn to our God, for he will forgive generously" (Isaiah 55:7).

Do you tend to wait several days before repenting of sin?

Do you really believe that God delights in you?

Is there someone in your life that avoids eye contact or deep conversations?

Who do you know that needs to delight?

As I look for the one who needs to delight, how do I become more like Jesus?

13

Looking For The One
WHO NEEDS A GUIDE

*"We are saved to serve; we are redeemed to reproduce
spiritually; we are 'fished out of the miry clay' so
that we in turn may become fishers of men."*

Billy Graham

MY FRIEND AND MENTOR Tom Kohout used to take me fishing for crappies on the lakes around Alexandria. It was sometimes hard to focus on fishing with a cooler filled with chocolate, macadamia nuts, and salted beef. But on this day, I was trying to keep up with our fishing guide. Mark was reeling in crappie after crappie and leaving me in the dust. I knew it wasn't the equipment. We used the same rods, reels, fishing lines, and jigs. It wasn't the location since we were sitting next to each other.

I finally asked Mark, "How come you catch five times as many crappies as I do?" Mark nodded toward his fishing rod.

"Because I watch the line."

When Mark saw the blank expression on my face, his voice grew quiet. "There are times when a crappie strikes a jig that you can't feel the vibration. You can't feel it, but you can see it." As I watched Mark's line, there was an almost imperceptible vibration. Mark set the hook!

Moments like this are why I love fishing. Nothing compares to casting for bass at sunset or reeling in a walleye on a beautiful fall day. But fishing is more than catching fish. There is always something new to discover or memories to treasure. I enjoy sorting tackle boxes and cleaning my reels. Most of all, I love the friendships that develop in a fishing boat.

Because I love to fish, I look for any excuse to stop by tackle stores. The superstores like Bass Pro are interesting, but the real magic happens in rural areas. I felt prompted to stop at a bait store in Western Minnesota one day. An older man was alone in the store and slumped behind the cash register. I quickly found out that he had spent decades as a fishing guide. When I tried to make conversation, I discovered that he was a man of few words. Despite the silence, I began to sense the presence of God. It was time to go fishing for a man on God's heart.

When you encounter someone on God's heart, you need insight into their heart. In this case, my first "cast" was to ask some questions about the churches in town. No interest. No nibble. I asked a question about his family, and the conversation quickly died down. I am all out of ideas, so I asked the fisher of men what to do. Once again, the still small voice of the Holy Spirit. "Ask about the depth finder."

There was a new depth finder on display, and as I asked questions, the guide described some of its features. I placed my hand on the depth finder. "When you are fishing, what is most important? What you can see or what you cannot see?" In the quiet, I noticed the gurgling of the water pump keeping the minnows alive for the first time.

The old guide thought for a moment. "Lots of people focus on what they can see. The shoreline, or the waves, but the secret is what's below the water. It's what you can't see."

"I have a question for you. If there is more to life than what we can see, would you want to know? Would you want to see and understand the spiritual world you can't see?" There was an even longer silence as the guide ran his fingers across his stubbled face.

Now instead of watching a fishing line, I was watching his face. It was almost imperceptible, but I saw something in his eyes. He quietly said, "I might be open to that." In the next several minutes, I shared about the life of Jesus and how many of his followers were fishermen. Jesus guided them to the fish, and he even made a shore lunch!

I shared that Jesus invited fishermen to follow him because he desired a relationship with them. He was offering to be their guide. Then we talked about his death on the cross and the offer of salvation.

As I studied his face, it was quiet again. He was deep in thought, and then a cloud came over his eyes. He slowly shook his head. Perhaps a memory or a fear was greater than his curiosity or hunger. I knew that I would begin to push him away from a commitment to Christ if I continued. So I thanked him and promised that I would be praying for him. I left him information about the radio station.

There are times when someone immediately surrenders their life to Jesus. It is like picking a piece of ripe fruit. There are many other times when your role is to plant a seed. The Apostle Paul shared, "I planted the seed in your hearts, and Apollos watered it, but it was God who made it grow" (1 Corinthians 3:6).

Paul knew that sharing the gospel was not about someone responding to him. Paul's passion was to plant the seed of the gospel in someone's heart. He knew that only God could make it grow.

This is why looking for the one is not a program or a speech or pressing people for decisions so that we can take the credit. Looking for the one is finding the one on God's heart. We search for a man's face in a tackle store because God searches for his heart. You are sensitive to the heart because the seed is planted in our hearts.

If we believe that our job is to press for commitments to Christ, we risk the gospel becoming a transaction. Our focal point is a prayer or a box checked on a card. We risk involving our pride in how many decisions for Christ we can report to our friends. We risk wounding a heart. But the Apostle Paul has a radically different way of looking at the gospel.

"It's not important who does the planting, or who does the watering. What's important is that God makes the seed grow. The one who plants and the one who waters work together with the same purpose. And both will be rewarded for their own hard work" (1 Corinthians 3:7-8).

REFLECT:

Am I involved in planting and watering the seed of the gospel?

Who am I guiding to Jesus?

EQUIP:

How do I look for the one who needs a guide?

FOLLOW JESUS: Here the cry of Jesus, "Come follow me, and I will show you how to fish for people" (Matthew 4:19). Recognize that to follow Jesus is to give him control of your life. "Let God have your life; He can do more with it than you can" (D.L. Moody).

STUDY PEOPLE: If you have good equipment, you'll catch fish. But you hire a fishing guide because you want to catch more fish. The guide knows where the hot spots are, and they have the latest equipment. But the biggest reason you want a guide in your boat is that fishing guides study fish. Like bass and northern pike, some fish are known for their aggression. When they strike a spinnerbait or a plastic worm, you know it. Most of the time, panfish are easy to catch. But walleye are a different story. I've enjoyed a few days when the walleye are actively feeding, but you have to be patient most days. On days when nothing was happening on Lake Reno, my dad would always say, "Let's slow down." When we slowed our speed or switched to a smaller bait, the walleye would often begin to bite.

SLOW DOWN: As followers of Jesus, we are called to be fishers of men, which means we need to slow down and see the people around us. Instead of judging lost people, we love lost people. Instead of yelling, we focus on listening. Instead of barricading our homes, we open our homes.

LOWER THE NETS: When you go fishing with Jesus, he sometimes directs you to places that make no sense. In those moments remember that Jesus is in the boat with you. Because he knows where the fish are, he knows precisely when and where to lower the nets.

LET'S PRAY:

Jesus, thank you for fishing me out of the miry clay and the joy of going fishing with you. Forgive me for slipping so easily from compassion to criticism. Forgive me for thinking of the gospel as dispensing information. Please help me be aware of your presence as I share about you. Open my eyes and my heart to the one on your heart.

DISCUSS:

Why do we guide someone to Jesus?

"I myself will tend my sheep and give them a place to lie down in peace, says the Sovereign Lord. I will search for my lost ones who strayed away, and I will bring them safely home again. I will bandage the injured and strengthen the weak" (Ezekiel 34:15-16).

How does sharing your life with someone serve to guide their life?

"We loved you so much that we shared with you not only God's Good News but our own lives, too" (1 Thessalonians 2:8).

How does God's Word guide us?

"All Scripture is inspired by God and is useful to teach us what is true and to make us realize what is wrong in our

> *lives. It corrects us when we are wrong and teaches us to do*
> *what is right. God uses it to prepare and equip his people to*
> *do every good work"* (2 Timothy 3:16-17).

What are some of the ways that Jesus shows us how to fish for people?

When sharing the gospel, what are some of the signs that you are pushing someone away from Christ? What do you watch for?

When you think of sharing the gospel, do you picture a monologue or a conversation?

As I look for the one who needs a guide, how do I become more like Jesus?

Looking For The One
WHO NEEDS A DEFENDER

*"For their Defender is strong; he will
take up their case against you."*

Proverbs 23:11, NIV

"I WANT YOU TO KNOW that I am innocent." I turned to see who had spoken and looked into the eyes of someone that I instantly believed. Charlie was a prisoner at Prairie Correctional Facility, and we were meeting after the prison's weekly chapel service. Charlie told me that he listened for hours every day to our radio ministry on KCGN and then walked away to his cell. But his words stayed with me on the long drive home. "I want you to know that I am innocent." He said it so matter-of-factly. He said it with such conviction.

Charlie began to write letters and open up about life at the prison. On the plus side, he was able to work. The downside was making only a few cents per hour. Charlie almost always included a gift with his letters, and I did the math. Based on his hourly pay Charlie was one of our most sacrificial donors.

As the letters continued, he shared the pain of being falsely accused and losing everything. Charlie had lost his marriage and his business. Someone had shattered his reputation, and now he had no money left to defend himself.

One sleepless night, Charlie sat on his bed face to face with his hopelessness. As Charlie thought about ending his life, the song, "You Raise Me Up" by Selah, came on his radio.

> "When I am down, and, oh, my soul, so weary
> When troubles come, and my heart burdened be
> Then, I am still and wait here in the silence
> Until you come and sit awhile with me
> You raise me up, so I can stand on mountains
> You raise me up to walk on stormy seas
> I am strong when I am on your shoulders
> You raise me up to more than I can be."

Charlie was overcome with the presence of God and began to weep. Then he began to rejoice. Somehow, someway, Jesus was going to raise him up. Then he knew how it was going to happen. He would appoint Jesus to be his defender.

The following letter was stunning. New evidence had emerged, and it had come to light that the person who had accused Charlie had accused multiple people of the same crime. A few months later, Charlie was a free man.

On the day of his release, a friend picked him up, and they headed for his hometown in Wisconsin. As they drove along in the dark, Charlie pondered something. How could he face all the people who believed that he was guilty? How could he even walk down the street?

It was late at night when they arrived in town, but something strange was happening downtown. The streets were empty, but there was one parking lot filled with cars, and it was the store that Charlie used to own. Charlie wondered aloud if a special event like Moonlight Madness was taking place. His friend proposed a crazy idea. "Charlie—I think you should stop by your store. I know you're worried about seeing everyone again. Why not just walk in and get it over with." Charlie hesitated, but something told him to stop running and start walking. He took a deep breath and opened the car door.

As Charlie walked into his store, he saw decorations, and then he noticed a crowd of people. When he saw their smiles and heard the applause, he realized that this gathering was in his honor. He realized that his defender had set him free and restored his reputation. Jesus had kept his promise to raise him up.

Charlie's life reminds me of a prisoner named Joseph, who was falsely accused. Joseph had no way of defending himself, "But the Lord was with Joseph in the prison and showed him his faithful love" (Genesis 39:21). As Joseph and Charlie discovered, our God can move quickly! "Then Pharaoh sent and called Joseph, and they quickly brought him out of the pit" (Genesis 41:14, ESV).

Charlie's life as a truck driver is not easy. Several months ago, he left me a voice message from a laundromat. He was alone in a strange town. It was late at night and yet he was thanking God for being so good to him. Instead of resenting prison, Charlie is thankful for prison. When he had absolutely nothing, Jesus came and found him.

Jesus came and revealed himself as his defender.

Someone that you know needs a defender. Their guilt is so great that they understand how King David felt when he said, "Wash me clean from my guilt. Purify me from my sin. For I recognize my rebellion; it haunts me day and night" (Psalm 51:2-3). Someone you know is sitting in a prison of guilt, and they have no hope.

When you are around this friend or family member, you may have noticed that they avoid eye contact. They have learned to keep their distance from the whispers and stares. They probably believe that if Jesus were to walk into the room, he would keep his distance from them.

The gospel of John paints a different picture. Jesus was teaching in the temple when a woman caught in the act of adultery was brought before him. The text does not specify, but I wonder how her accusers treated her. Was she gently brought before Jesus, or was she hurled at his feet? The price tag for her sin is evident in Old Testament law. The Pharisees said, "The law of Moses says to stone her. What do you say?" (John 8:5)

This woman has no defense, but she has a defender.

Jesus begins his defense by stooping down and writing in the dust with his finger. By the way, have you ever wondered what he was writing in the dust? During one of my Bible classes at Bethel University, Dr. Wayne Gruden posed this question. "I wonder if he began to write the names of women that the Pharisees had slept with?" We don't know what Jesus was writing, but when the words were written, Jesus stood to his feet and raised his voice. "'All right, but let the one who has never sinned throw the first stone!' Then he stooped down again and wrote in the dust" (John 8:7-8).

Close your eyes and imagine that you are the one caught in sin. You hear the accusations, and you see the feet of those who have gathered to take your life. Imagine the terror as you wait for the impact of the first stone. Then you see a man kneeling beside you. You see his finger writing words in the dust. And then you hear it. The sound of rocks falling to the ground. The sound of footsteps fading into the distance. Now the sweetest sound of all. "Where are your accusers? Didn't even one of them condemn you?" (John 8:10)

Hear her whisper, "No, Lord."

Now imagine the face of Jesus as he says, "Neither do I. Go and sin no more" (John 8:11).

This woman and Charlie have something in common. They both discovered that the first step in our defense is to be defenseless.

We have no defense for our sin, but we have a defender.

REFLECT:

Where do I need a defender?

EQUIP:

How do I look for the one who needs a defender?

ASK FOR A REVELATION: If you tend to see the sin around you through critical eyes, it is because you see yourself through critical eyes. Ask Jesus for a revelation of how he sees you. Now ask Jesus to help you see people through his eyes. When you see a sinner through the eyes of Jesus, they step closer to you most of the time. As they step closer to you, they step closer to him. The look in your eyes and the tone of your voice is so different from their accusers. They feel safe around you. As you share about the mercy of Jesus, they hear the sound of falling rocks. As you share the plan of salvation, they receive their defender.

John's account of this story includes this insight: As the accusers slipped away into the crowd "only Jesus was left in the middle of the crowd with the woman" (John 8:9).

Only Jesus can save us.

Only Jesus can make us new.

REPENTANCE: Is there something that haunts you day and night? Instead of defending yourself, take a moment to kneel in repentance. Realize at this moment that you are not alone. The one kneeling beside you is Jesus, and he is writing words of hope in the dust of your life. As the rocks of guilt and shame fall to the ground, hear his whisper, "Where are your accusers?" As his love washes over you, hear his invitation. "Go and sin no more."

Is there someone in my life that needs to hear the same whisper?

LET'S PRAY:

Jesus, come and sweep away my critical spirit toward sinful people. I've labeled and judged, but now I stand beside them at the foot of the cross. I confess that I have sinned and fallen short of your glory. My only hope is you. Prepare my heart and anoint my eyes to look for the one who needs a defender, and give me the courage to kneel beside them.

DISCUSS:

Do you tend to be critical of yourself?

Do you tend to be critical of the people around you?

When you fail, how do you think Jesus responds to you?

Who are some of the people we are called to defend?

"Defend the weak and the fatherless; uphold the cause of the poor and the oppressed" (Psalm 82:3, NIV).

"Learn to do good. Seek justice. Help the oppressed. Defend the cause of orphans. Fight for the rights of widows" (Isaiah 1:17).

How does Jesus feel about the defenseless?

How does looking for the one who needs a defender make me more like Jesus?

Looking For The One
WHO NEEDS TO BE SURE

"As she listened to us, the Lord opened her heart."

Acts 16:14

"WHAT'S THE GOOD WORD for today?"

The smiling face behind the words was Peg Imhoff. This remarkable woman had served as the Minnesota Twins Press Box Ambassador for over 40 years and was known and loved around major league baseball. Bert Blyleven beamed when he saw Peg and brought her treats to brighten her day. Peg went into the locker room to give Coach Paul Molitor a hug when the team was struggling.

Peg asked what the good word was on Sunday mornings, and it was my delight to share a condensed version from the chapel message for the Twins players with her. If members of the media were nearby, she enthusiastically said, "Come here. You need to hear this!"

One of my favorite Peg stories is from 1987. It is game 7 of the World Series, and Peg leaves for her home during the 7th inning because "I always leave during the 7th inning. Why get caught in traffic?" As Peg arrives home and is watching the last inning, it suddenly dawns on her. She has the key to the cooler that holds the champagne! Peg rushes back downtown in time for the postgame celebration. Peg once commented to me, "Where else can you work where you can be kissed on the cheek by Harmon Killebrew?"

One Sunday morning, I shared with Peg that one of the players had given his life to Christ during chapel. "He had heard about God but never really knew Jesus."

Peg quietly said, "When it's my time to go, I hope I make it through the pearly gates." There was something about the look on Peg's face. There was a question in her eyes.

"Peg, are you sure that you are going to heaven?"

Peg laughed, "Well, I need all the help I can get. My husband told me that he would leave a rope through the pearly gates, and if there were any trouble, he would pull me through."

I knelt by her desk and said, "Peg, you don't have to wonder. Would you like to be sure that you are going to heaven?" Peg looked into my eyes and nodded her head. We talked for a moment about 1 John 5:13: "I have written this to you who believe in the name of the Son of God, so that you may know you have eternal life." "Peg, would you like to invite Jesus to be your Savior? Would you like to be sure of your salvation?"

My dear friend said, "Yes."

As I shared some verses and The Salvation Poem, Peg bowed her head and invited Jesus to be her Savior, Lord, and Friend. A few days later, I stopped by to see Peg and her face was somber. "I want you to be among the first to know. I just found out that I have cancer. I don't have long to live."

Peg did not have long to live and, within a few days, was hospitalized. When Sherrie and I stopped by to pray with her, her face was full of peace as she asked me a question. "Dave, would you do my funeral? I want my friends and co-workers to know about my commitment to Christ." Then we shared communion with Peg.

The Twins graciously offered to host Peg's funeral service at Target Field. It took my breath away to see Peg's picture on the center-field scoreboard as I arrived. There were beautiful tributes from members of the media and former players. Peg's dear friend Sue is the Twins organist and played beautifully at the service. Peg's children shared about getting tucked into bed—knowing that Mom would then go downstairs and spend hours repairing their old home. Peg's standards were clear. There was no money for soft drinks, no chewing with your mouth open, and no hats at the table. Manners mattered.

I remembered Peg telling me about a time at the stadium when a well-known sportswriter walked up in the media center and said, "I'll have a hot dog." She smiled at him but didn't lift a finger. After a long pause, she said, "I'm waiting for you to say please."

After many beautiful tributes, I shared Peg's story of accepting Jesus and her request to share the gospel at her funeral. The crowd grew quiet as they heard the good news that you can know Jesus and be sure of salvation. I shared a verse that I had read to Peg. "When God our Savior revealed his kindness and love, he saved us, not because of the righteous things we had done, but because of his mercy" (Titus 3:4-5).

A few days after the funeral, I remembered a conversation with Peg several years ago. Peg shared that in 2013 Yankees closer Mariano Rivera was making his last visit to Target Field. As a future Hall of Famer, the Twins honored him with a tribute that included a rocking chair made from broken bats. As part of his farewell tour, Mariano asked the Twins to gather some long-time staff members so that he could speak personally to them. Peg said he thanked them for their service and for being a part of his life. Her eyes grew wide as she added, "Then he shared about his faith in Christ. He said that his faith was the most important thing in his life."

Looking for the one is almost always a team effort. You might be in a one-on-one conversation, but you are not alone. God in his mercy has been reaching out to this one, and only He can bring them to life. The Apostle Paul observed, "I planted the seed in your hearts, and Apollos watered it, but it was God who made it grow" (1 Corinthians 3:6).

As I thought about Peg's meeting with Mariano in 2013, I was thunderstruck. The greatest closer in the history of baseball served as the setup man for the salvation of Peg Imhoff. How amazing!

REFLECT:

Are you hoping for heaven, or are you sure of your salvation?

Is there someone in your life who is not sure?

EQUIP:

How do I look for the one who is unsure?

POINT OF DECISION: As Jesus met people, he brought them to the point of decision. Jesus asked Peter, "'Who do you say that I am?' Peter answered him, 'You are the Christ, the son of the living God'" (Matthew 16:15-16). Jesus asked a direct question because he knew that Peter had to answer the question for himself. As a missionary who gave his life for the gospel, Jim Elliot lifted this prayer. "Lord, make me a crisis man. Let me not be a milepost on a single road, but make me a fork in the road that people must turn one way or another in facing Christ in me."

JESUS OPENS HEARTS: If you are hesitant to share your faith, it might be because you are taking responsibility for someone's response to Jesus. Paul and Silas shared the good news in Philippi with a merchant of expensive purple cloth named Lydia. Their summary of her response is beautiful. "As she listened to us, the Lord opened her heart, and she accepted what Paul was saying" (Acts 16:14).

ASK QUESTIONS: Here are some questions that can bring someone to a fork in the road:

Q: If your life were to end today, do you know that you are going to heaven?

Q: Do you ever worry that you've not done enough good things to get into heaven?

Q: Do you believe it is possible to know if you are going to heaven?

Q: Would you like to be sure of your salvation?

LET'S PRAY:

Jesus, there are people around me who are not sure that they know you—because they do not know you. Without you, I can't see the uncertainty hidden in their hearts. I can't see it unless you open my eyes so I ask you for supernatural discernment. I make myself available as the setup person or the closer because only you can open a heart and bring someone to life! As I look for the one who is not sure, help me become more like you.

DISCUSS:

Can you recall a decision for Christ in your life?

Is there someone in your life who needs to be sure about their salvation?

What are some of the benefits of knowing we are saved?

"But let us who live in the light be clearheaded, protected by the armor of faith and love, and wearing as our helmet the confidence of our salvation" (1 Thessalonians 5:8).

What is our certain hope?

"For the Lord himself will come down from heaven with a commanding shout, with the voice of the archangel, and with the trumpet call of God. First, the believers who have died will rise from their graves. Then, together with them, we who are still alive and remain on the earth will be caught up in the clouds to meet the Lord in the air. Then we will be with the Lord forever. So encourage each other with these words" (1 Thessalonians 4:16-18).

Did you find Jesus or did Jesus find you?

"Behold, God is my salvation; I will trust, and will not be afraid; for the Lord God is my strength and my song, and he has become my salvation" (Isaiah 12:2).

As I look for the one who needs to be sure, how do I become more like Jesus?

16

Looking For The One
WHO NEEDS THE BLESSING

*"Esau pleaded, 'But do you have only one blessing? Oh my
father, bless me, too!' Then Esau broke down and wept."*

Genesis 27:38

AS THE OLDER MAN stepped onto the airport shuttle, I had to
smile. His weather-beaten hands and face spoke of a life of hard
work. His frayed suit and tie hinted that he was leaving on an
important trip. We waited on the Park 'N Fly shuttle for several minutes, but since there were no other passengers, it was just the two of
us as we headed to the airport for our departure flights.

As I thought, this man had spent a lifetime farming. He was
quiet, but he began to open up as we talked about the weather and
the crops. Then I asked why he was wearing a suit and tie.

His eyes lit up as he quietly said, "It's for my daughter."

For the next several minutes, he told me all about his daughter.
Despite growing up on a farm near a small town, her dream was to
play in a symphony orchestra. As a teenager, she had spent countless
hours practicing the violin. He recalled hearing her violin coming
from her bedroom window on hot summer days. His eyes filled with
emotion as he shared how she had worked to help pay for college.
He described a girl who refused to let go of her dream.

Now she played for an orchestra on the East Coast and had just been chosen for a special honor. This hard-working farmer was all dressed up in his Sunday best as he traveled east to honor her. The look on his face said it all. He loved and treasured his daughter.

A week later, I flew back to the Twin Cities and once again made my way down to the Park 'N Fly shuttles. I was relieved to see the shuttle arriving on time, and as I took my seat, an older man was walking toward the shuttle. There was something familiar about him. Then it dawned on me. The older man was the farmer, but he was not alone this time. Walking next to him was a woman.

As they sat down, we laughed about the "coincidence" of our flights and even our shuttle rides matching up. He said, "I would like to introduce you to my daughter." I turned my attention to this well-dressed woman, and as we met, I noticed her hands—the beautiful hands of an artist.

"Are you the daughter who plays the violin?"

She looked at me with puzzled eyes. "How do you know about the violin?"

"Because on the shuttle to the airport, your dad told me all about the violin. He told me all about you."

Now her face registered astonishment. "Dad—what were you saying about me?" In the silence, he shrugged his shoulders and carefully studied his hands.

When you look for the one, there are times when the God "appointments" are hard to discern. You don't know, "Is this the one?" There are other times when there is no doubt.

She turned to her Father, and this time the question was filled with urgency. "Daddy, what did you tell him about me?"

As the question hung in the air, I looked into her eyes, and then I understood. The question mattered because she longed to know what her father thought about her. She longed to have his blessing.

The concept of the blessing is found throughout God's Word. One of the best-known examples is the story of Jacob and Esau and their father Isaac.

"One day, when Isaac was old and turning blind, he called for Esau, his older son, and said, 'My son.' 'Yes, Father?' Esau replied. 'I am an old man now,' Isaac said, 'and I don't know when I may die. Take your bow and a quiver full of arrows, and go out into the open country to hunt some wild game for me. Prepare my favorite dish, and bring it here for me to eat. Then I will pronounce the blessing that belongs to you, my firstborn son before I die'" (Genesis 27:1-4).

Isaac's wife, Rebekah, overhears this conversation and convinces Jacob to pretend to be his older brother and receive the special blessing that belonged to Esau. The plan works to perfection. Isaac blesses Jacob, asking God to give him abundant harvests and declaring, "May many nations become your servant, may they bow down to you" (Genesis 27:28-29). All is well until Esau arrives home and discovers his Father has been deceived and his blessing stolen. His cry echoes across time, "'Oh my Father, what about me? Bless me, too!' he begged" (Genesis 27:34).

There are people all around us who have never received the blessing. They don't know who they are or their purpose because no one has spoken the blessing of God over them. Their God-given blessing has been stolen by the evil one. But our redeemer can restore the blessing. Our God arranges shuttle schedules so that a daughter receives the blessing of her father.

As the daughter turned from her father and looked at me, I said, "I pray each day that Jesus will show me one person on his heart.

One person he wants to bless. Today, you are that person. Jesus wants you to know how your father feels about you.

"Your dad loves you and is so proud of you. He loved you as a little girl when you told him about your dream of playing the violin. We talked about all of the lessons and years of hard work. All of the times when you could have given up but refused to. He told me about the extra jobs during college and the day when your dream finally came true. He shared with me about your award.

"Your dad may not have felt comfortable saying it to you, but he said it to me. Your dad loves you. You have his blessing."

As we pulled into the parking lot, the father glanced up at me. As he turned to leave, he mumbled, "Thanks a lot."

His daughter helped him off the shuttle, and they strolled toward their vehicle. Then the daughter, with the beautiful hands and tears running down her face, ran back to the shuttle. As she held my hands, she said, "Thank you!"

REFLECT:

Do the people you love have your blessing?

EQUIP:

How do I look for the one who needs the blessing?

RECEIVE A BLESSING: Before speaking a blessing, you need to receive a blessing. You may never receive the blessing from your mom or dad, but your Heavenly Father has a blessing for you. He is the God who loves you with an "everlasting love" (Jeremiah 31:3). He is the God who declares, "'For I know the plans I have for you,' says the Lord. 'They are plans for good and not for disaster, to give you a future and a hope.'" (Jeremiah 29:11). As you receive the blessing, you are equipped to speak a blessing.

A friend of mine pastors a church. At an evening service, they were impressed that each person had an opportunity to receive the blessing. As the service closed, you were invited to stand in front of a mirror and declare from Psalm 139, "I am fearfully and wonderfully made." An older woman came forward, but she was silent when she stood in front of the mirror. Instead of looking into the mirror, her eyes were locked on the floor. In the quiet, several friends stood around her and began to speak words of life. They knew her family history and the battle that was taking place. As expressions of blessing flowed, she dared to slowly lift her head and declare, "I am fearfully and wonderfully made!" You can receive the blessing by proclaiming God's word in your prayer closet or when your friends discern it is time to gather around you.

BLESSING OUR CHILDREN: When our son Kyle was around fifteen years old, I sensed he was going through a season of deep discouragement. As we talked one night, the problem was not something happening to Kyle. The issue was within Kyle. He felt like a failure. I pulled out a legal pad and asked Kyle to share some of the good things in his life or something he was good at. There was a long silence. "The only thing I'm good at is golf, and right now, I'm terrible." As a dad, it was my honor to lift Kyle's eyes to help him see God's design in him. We made a list of attributes that had nothing to do with golf and everything to do with his divine design. In *The Blessing*, Gary Smalley shares, "Affirming words from moms and dads are like light switches. Speak a word of affirmation at the right moment in a child's life, and it's like lighting up a whole roomful of possibilities."

As a mom or dad, you can fill your home with moments that bless or moments that tear down. Your children know what is wrong with them, but your role is to communicate what is right. In our home, Sherrie came up with the idea of "honor night." Almost every Friday night, Sherrie made her special homemade pizza. After dinner, we would go around the table and honor one person. There were weeks when our three sons were not in the mood to bless one another. There were weeks when it was holy ground.

My friend Gordy is so intentional about the blessing that every summer he hosts a family gathering where he blesses each child and grandchild. He wondered as his grandchildren became teenagers if they would resist moments like this, but so far no one wants to miss Grandpa's blessing.

If your son or daughter feels that you disapprove of them, a typical response is to reject what matters most to you. If your son or daughter feels you are blessing them, it is natural to embrace what matters most to you. As you bless your children may this be your testimony. "I could have no greater joy than to hear that my children are following the truth" (3 John 4).

May you receive the blessing so that you can release it into your home or even an airport shuttle!

LET'S PRAY:

Father, forgive me for calling unworthy what you call blessed. Forgive me for resisting your unconditional love. As I receive my blessing from you, I pray that you will open my eyes to the one who needs the blessing. Now I pray in faith, "Oh, that you would bless me and expand my territory! Please be with me in all that I do, and keep me from all trouble and pain!" (1 Chronicles 4:10) Anoint me to see people through your eyes. Equip me to bless and build! As I look for the one who needs the blessing, make me more like Jesus.

DISCUSS:

Were you raised in a home where you received the blessing?

Do you tend to focus on failures and faults?

Does God focus on our failures and faults?

"If any of you lacks wisdom, you should ask God, who gives generously to all without finding fault, and it will be given to you" (James 1:5, NIV).

How does your focus on the past hinder your ability to move forward?

"But one thing I do: forgetting what lies behind and straining forward to what lies ahead, I press on toward the goal for the prize of the upward call of God in Christ Jesus" (Philippians 3:13-14, ESV).

Do you find forgiveness difficult, or do you have the grace that "keeps no record of being wronged?" (1 Corinthians 13:5)

Is it possible that your relationships are being shaped by the whisper in your heart that you are not enough?

As I look for the one who needs the blessing, how do I become more like Jesus?

17

Looking For The One
WHO FEELS UNWORTHY

*"I am overwhelmed with joy in the Lord my God! For he
has dressed me with the clothing of salvation and draped
me in a robe of righteousness. I am like a bridegroom
dressed for his wedding or a bride with her jewels."*

Isaiah 61:10

THE ENGINE IN MY OLD CAR groaned as it came to life. The temperature was well below zero, and as I waited for the engine to warm up, I was discouraged. "Father, I thought I heard from you. Why was there no response?"

I had been asked to speak at a women's event in Brooten, Minnesota, with ladies in attendance from several area churches. It had been a wonderful evening with a church basement filled with laughter and homemade pie.

When asked to share at any gathering, I wait before the Lord and ask him to show me who will be in attendance and what He wants to speak to their heart. I have had times when I know in a few minutes; other times, I have waited for days to finally sense what direction to take the message.

On this occasion, I had a picture of a woman who felt unloved in the hidden places of her heart. She felt unwanted and ashamed. She felt unworthy. As I saw her heart, it broke my heart.

After a delicious meal, I shared what it was like to grow up on a farm and watch my mom and dad hanging by a thread from the financial stress. Night after night, they would sit in the kitchen, trying to find a way to pay the bills. What they didn't know was that the sound of their voices carried their pain and fear to my bedroom.

Alone in the dark, I believed several lies: I would never be able to provide for a family. No one could know me and still love me. I felt unworthy and unacceptable.

I spoke about the fire that destroyed our dairy barn and my dad's injuries when his leg was caught in an auger.

Then I shared the wonder of looking over on a Sunday morning and seeing Sherrie for the first time. She was worshipping Jesus, and the look on her face took my breath away. My friends Gary and Vicki set up our first date, and the four of us got together for an evening of board games and brownies. I took a deep breath, asking her out for a second date where I decided that I would find out what she believed about topics like healing, worship, and the Church. Somehow Sherrie saw past my unusual approach to romance, and we began to fall in love.

As our love grew, I started to back away because of my fear that I could never provide or be entirely accepted. Finally, I opened up about the night when I prayed well past midnight, and the presence of God swept away my fear.

On July 14th, 1984, I stood at the altar, waiting for my bride, and Sherrie was worth the wait. Our photographer captured her beautiful smile as our eyes met as she came down the aisle. As we turned to share our vows, I remembered a wedding I had attended a few years earlier. The groom was unwilling to make eye contact with his bride during the vows. He would glance at her but not look at her. But on this day, my wedding day, all I saw was Sherrie.

We made our vows and said, "I do," and then faced our family and friends as Pastor Reishus introduced us for the first time as Mr. and Mrs. David McIver. We had entered the sanctuary as two separate people who were now joined together as one flesh.

There was a hush in the church basement as I pulled out an 8x10 picture from our wedding day and asked the question: "Have you said 'I do'?"

I shared from God's Word the beautiful imagery of salvation as an invitation to be the bride of Christ. "For I am jealous for you with the jealously of God himself. I promised you as a pure bride to one husband—Christ" (2 Corinthians 11:2).

Warren Wiersbe helps us understand the imagery of the bride. "The picture here is that of a loving father who has a daughter engaged to be married. He feels it is his privilege and duty to keep her pure so that he can present her to the husband with joy and not with sorrow. Paul saw the local church as a bride, engaged to be married to Jesus Christ."

"You see, you can know about Jesus and even 'date' him, but that is not the same as pledging your life to him. If you are married this evening, you know precisely when you said, 'I do.' But, can you remember a moment when you said 'I do' to Jesus?"

At the close of the service, I gave an invitation. "Imagine for a moment that Jesus is here, but you feel unworthy. He looks at you, but you don't dare look at him. But instead of looking away or walking away, he lifts your face to his face. Then he says: 'You see the broken places and the failures, but I see your heart. I see you, I love you, and I want you to be my bride. I promise to love you with everlasting love. Will you turn from your sin and return to me? Will you say, "I do"?'"

Now, as I shivered in the car, I thought about the close of the service. There were conversations about the food and the weather, but not one person had committed to Christ. Had I missed the Lord? It was a long drive home across the frozen roads.

About ten years later, I was standing in a country grocery store when a voice behind me said, "I was there the night you asked us to say, 'I do.'" I turned and saw eyes that burned with fire. "I had gone to church my whole life but never committed my life to Christ. That night I said, 'I do.'"

With that, she turned and walked away.

REFLECT:

Have you said "I do" to Jesus?

EQUIP:

How do I look for the one who feels unworthy?

THE WORTHY ONE: This is not an invitation to a self-help seminar. We are inviting someone to meet the one who gave his life. The one who is worthy. "Worthy is the Lamb who was slaughtered—to receive power and riches and wisdom and strength and honor and glory and blessing" (Revelation 5:12).

RECEIVE YOUR IDENTITY: When you are adopted by Jesus Christ, he replaces lies with truth. You are stepping into the light. As you spend time in God's Word, you replace lies with truth and you are able to fulfill your destiny. "There is no escaping your identity.

You will not live beyond how you see yourself" (John Eldredge).

FIGHT FOR FREEDOM: If you begin to lose heart, consider what is at stake. The fight for your freedom is essential for those you are called to set free. As you refuse to give up, as you press in to pray, this is your declaration: "I prayed to the Lord, and he answered me. He freed me from all my fears. Those who look to him for help will be radiant with joy; no shadow of shame will darken their faces" (Psalm 34:4-5).

Somewhere, there is a woman in a church basement waiting for you to come and set her free. Because of your pain, you perceive her pain. As she says, "I do," you see eyes that burn with fire!

HOLD A BANQUET: Do you know someone who feels unwanted and ashamed? Consider how intentional Jesus was in reaching out to those who were considered unworthy: "Later, Levi held a banquet in his home with Jesus as the guest of honor. Many of Levi's fellow tax collectors and other guests also ate with them. But the Pharisees and their teachers of religious law complained bitterly to Jesus' disciples, 'Why do you eat and drink with such scum?' Jesus answered them, 'Healthy people don't need a doctor—sick people do. I have come to call not those who think they are righteous, but those who know they are sinners and need to repent'" (Luke 5:29-32).

LET'S PRAY:

Jesus, I have wrestled with my shame and guilt and felt so unworthy of you. I've been alone in the dark. But you were never far away. Please show me any lie that I am still believing. In the process of setting me free, make my life a vessel of grace. May your love bring light to my eyes. Now open my eyes to the one who feels unworthy. Clear my heart of any critical spirit to what they have done, and show me how to share my brokenness with them. Order my steps so that they can walk with you. As I look for the one who feels unworthy, make me more like Jesus.

DISCUSS:

What are some of the reasons that you feel unworthy?

Are these reasons greater than God's ability to restore and redeem you?

"So now there is no condemnation for those who belong to Christ Jesus. And because you belong to him, the power of the life-giving Spirit has freed you from the power of sin that leads to death" (Romans 8:1-2).

What did Jesus cancel on the cross?

"He canceled the record of the charges against us and took it away by nailing it to the cross" (Colossians 2:14).

Why did God pay a ransom to save you?

"For you know that God paid a ransom to save you from the empty life you inherited from your ancestors. And it was not paid with mere gold or silver, which lose their value. It was the precious blood of Christ, the sinless, spotless Lamb of God" (1 Peter 1:18-19).

What is the difference between self worth and who we are in Christ?

"Therefore, if anyone is in Christ, he is a new creation. The old has passed away; behold, the new has come" (2 Corinthians 5:17).

Why does God want to adopt us?

"God decided in advance to adopt us into his own family by bringing us to himself through Jesus Christ. This is what he wanted to do, and it gave him great pleasure" (Ephesians 1:5).

As I look for the one who feels unworthy, how do I become more like Jesus?

Looking for the One
WHO IS ANGRY

*"All of the Father's white-hot anger against my sin
was poured out on the cross. Because of Jesus, the
Father has no anger left for you and me."*

Joni Eareckson-Tada

IT WAS A BEAUTIFUL Tuesday afternoon. As I drove to Whole Foods in downtown Minneapolis, I was thinking about the Bible study that had just concluded at Target Field. The men in this study play for the Minnesota Twins, and these men are honest. They ask great questions and challenge one another. They challenge me!

As I waited in line to buy my salad, a voice behind me asked a question. "So, what do you think of Gardy?"

As I turned around, I realized my stadium credential was still around my neck, and the man behind me had noticed the Twins Logo. I saw his Detroit Tigers T-Shirt, and then I noticed his eyes. The eyes were intense and probing. There was a question behind the question.

Gardy had coached the Twins for many years and was now coaching the Detroit Tigers. I quickly answered that I had a lot of respect for Ron Gardenhire's years with the Twins and hoped things went well with the Tigers. I sat down to eat my lunch, and the man with the Tigers jersey sat down next to me. I quickly realized that this was an answer to prayer.

As I walk into stores, I lift a life-changing prayer. "Lord, show me the one." If an older person needs help with their cart, they are the one. If someone is looking for a food item, we find it together. If young kids are out of control, I do what I can to come to the rescue. When approaching the checkout line, I whisper, "Lord, show me which line." I know from experience that the Lord often directs me to stand in the longest line.

As Doug sat down, he introduced himself and shared that he had flown into town for the Tigers series with the Twins. As a diehard Tigers fan, he thought nothing of investing thousands of dollars every year to watch his team on the road.

Then the conversation took an interesting turn. Doug began to share his spiritual background and search for a real relationship with God. Doug's voice grew tender as he shared about his daughter and her battle with alcohol. There were so many years of heartbreak and poor decisions. Then the welcome news that his daughter was finally free from her addiction.

Doug took a moment to compose himself. His daughter called to say that a party was taking place at a bar. She would be in attendance to honor her good friend. She promised her dad that she would not take one drink. She would be okay.

The next phone call came at 3:00 AM.

His daughter had lost control at the party, and on the way home, lost control of her vehicle. His daughter was dead. Doug showed me the picture of her young children seated on the grass around her tombstone. The look on their faces said it all.

We talked about pain and loss, and finally, I asked Doug if he had a relationship with Jesus.

"No, I don't. Just a lot of questions."

But Doug did not want to talk about Jesus. He wanted to discuss the medieval crusades and various leaders in the modern Church that he thought were off base. As Doug asked questions, I would turn the conversation back to Jesus because "Christ is the visible image of the invisible God" (Colossians 1:15).

We finally ran out of time, but then a thought came to me. "Go to the game with Doug." When I asked if I could join him at the game, he was delighted. It was a beautiful evening as Doug and I sat in the upper deck in right field. As the sun was setting, I asked Doug if he knew why Jesus had gone to the cross. I walked Doug through the gospel and the amazing truth that "He made peace with everything in heaven and on earth by means of Christ's blood on the cross" (Colossians 1:20).

Doug responded, "I still have questions about the crusades and the Church." Then the Holy Spirit changed a life by whispering a question. "Is the reason you want to talk about the sins of the Church because the Church wounded you?" There was a long silence, then Doug lowered his head and quietly shared what had happened during his childhood. He was honest about his pain and his anger toward God.

There were strikeouts and home runs that night, but the greater battle was in right field. Doug longed to know Jesus, but he associated him with the church that had harmed him as a young boy. He was angry at God for the death of his daughter. He had carried his pain and secrets for decades, but this night, as he experienced the love of Jesus, he finally told the truth. As the evening came to a close, I prayed with Doug and could see the beginning of hope on his face.

Now and then, I pull out my phone and look at the picture of Doug's children at the graveside of their mother. I pray for Doug's loss and anger. I think about the long and winding road he is still walking along. Then I give thanks to the God who whispers which line to get into and whispers questions that unlock a heart.

We pray about grocery store lines because eternity is at stake.

REFLECT:

Am I willing to look for the one who is angry?

There are many reasons why we keep our distance from angry people. We are keeping out of harm's way, or responding to anger with a critical spirit. But anger is also communicating something about the condition of the heart, and almost no one is looking for the one who is angry.

EQUIP:

How do I look for the one who is angry?

LISTENING: When looking for the one who is angry, a great place to begin is by listening and asking questions. Be careful of offering opinions and ideas because opinions and ideas rarely heal anger. Your goal is to peel away one layer at a time, and when the time is right, present the truth of who Jesus is. Your hope is a glimpse of Jesus.

ADDRESS GOD'S ANGER: Angry people often believe that God is angry. Specifically, that God is angry with them. God's response to our sin is indeed anger. "Don't be fooled by those who try to excuse these sins, for the anger of God will fall on all who disobey him"

(Ephesians 5:6). But, the angry one needs to know that as Jesus went to the cross, he drank the cup of God's wrath.

MAKE AN INTRODUCTION: As we present the good news of Jesus, it is an invitation to repent and receive Jesus as our sin-bearer. It is time for the angry one to meet the God who is no longer angry. "Jehovah's gracious eye never looks on you in anger when he looks at you through Christ, for then He sees no sin. Though you still struggle with sin, you are always accepted in Christ, always blessed, and always dear to the Father's heart" (Charles H. Spurgeon).

STAND YOUR GROUND: There are times when we need to run from danger. But most of the time, we need to stand our ground. The angry one has learned to use anger to manipulate and control. Or to excuse their sin. But their anger is not the center of their story. The one who drank the cup of God's anger is the center of their story. "God showed his great love for us by sending Christ to die for us while we were still sinners" (Romans 5:8).

As Christ's ambassador, you listen and ask great questions. You discern what the anger is really about, and then as the sun is setting, you present Jesus.

LET'S PRAY:

Jesus, I don't want to be around angry people. They make me feel uncomfortable. Sometimes they attack me. Sometimes they harm me. So I fix my eyes on you and remember that angry people attacked you. At the cross, you absorbed the angry cries of "Crucify him" as you absorbed the wrath of God for me. Would you please show me any anger in my heart that I can bring under your authority? Forgive me for using anger to manipulate or control people. Now open my eyes to the angry one. Anoint my words and even my gaze to gently peel away the layers. Help me to handle this fragile heart with care. All I can offer is a glimpse of Jesus because "He heals the brokenhearted and bandages their wounds" (Psalm 147:3). As I look for the one who is angry, help me become more like Jesus.

DISCUSS:

What is the difference between responding in anger and being controlled by anger?

"Don't sin by letting anger control you. Think about it overnight and remain silent" (Psalm 4:4).

Are you angry about something from your past?

"And don't sin by letting anger control you. Don't let the sun go down while you are still angry" (Ephesians 4:26).

How do you respond to angry people?

"A soft answer turns away wrath, but a harsh word stirs up anger" (Proverbs 15:1).

How do you discern what anger is really about?

Do you believe that God is angry with you?

As I look for the one who is angry, how do I become more like Jesus?

Looking For The One
WHO NEEDS AN INTERCESSOR

"There are two sorts of prayer: personal and intercessory. The latter ordinarily occupies the lesser part of our time and energy. This may not be. Christ has opened the school of prayer specially to train intercessors for the great work of bringing down, by their faith and prayer, the blessings of His work and love on the world around."

Andrew Murray

THE THIRD ROUND of the 1996 British Open is underway, and I am on my knees. Tom Lehman rolls in his putt on the 18th hole and has just fired a 64. He is in the lead heading into the final round of this major championship. I slowly stand to my feet and stretch my back. I have been on my knees for hours.

Then I think of the first day I prayed for Tom.

Several years earlier, I had just finished Andrew Murray's book, *With Christ in the School of Prayer.* As I read these words, I was stunned. "While we ordinarily first bring our own needs to God in prayer and then think of what belongs to God and His interests, the Master reverses the order. First, Thy name, Thy kingdom, Thy will; then give us, forgive us, lead us, deliver us..."

I have spent a lifetime bringing lists of what I need to God. My prayer life has been about my life. Now, a revelation that prayer is asking God what is on his heart. I saw for the first time that intercessory prayer is wrestling for what is on God's heart. This revelation immediately changed how I pray for my family and radio ministry.

In the early 1990s, I prayed one day, "Jesus, who is on your heart?"

I waited in the stillness; there was no audible voice, but a series of phrases came in rapid succession. "Tom Lehman is on my heart. I have called him to take the gospel to the ends of the earth, but he will not accomplish this without intercession. Principalities and powers are opposing him. I am asking you to tear down the strongholds and be a covering of prayer over his family. I am asking you to fight for him."

I was stunned. It was so clear and yet so unexpected. I had never met Tom but knew that he had struggled to keep his place on the PGA Tour for years. I knew Tom grew up in Alexandria, Minnesota. My friend Ed Christopherson had shared with me about Tom's decision for Christ at an FCA meeting.

When you look for the one and the Holy Spirit speaks to you, the following prayer takes your breath away. "Father, show me your heart for Tom." As soon as I prayed, I began to "see" Tom in various chapters of his life and felt the overwhelming love of God for him.

The next prayer was a delight: "Father, what do you want to do through his life?" Now there was another wave of revelation. I saw God's heart for Tom to ascend in the world of golf and share a particular message about the love of God on the PGA tour and to millions of people around the world.

Now that I knew God's heart for Tom's career, I needed to understand what opposed him. I needed to know how to fight for him.

The Bible tells us that we wrestle against spiritual forces. "For we do not wrestle against flesh and blood, but against the rulers, against the authorities, against the cosmic powers over this present darkness, against the spiritual forces of evil in the heavenly places" (Ephesians 6:12, ESV).

My high school career as a wrestler spanned exactly two matches. I took part in a wrestling tournament at Glenwood High School and somehow won my first match against another guy on the basketball team. Neither one of us had a clue how to wrestle. A few minutes later, my heart sank as my next opponent walked into the center of the floor. Daryl was not just an outstanding high school wrestler. He was also the son of the wrestling coach.

As the match began, Daryl graciously informed me that he would coach me during the first period and wait until the second period to pin me. There was no hint of trash talk or intimidation—just the quiet voice of a young man who had grown up in a wrestling family. In the first period, he whispered instructions about half nelsons and takedowns as we put on a good show for the crowd. In the second period, he was all business. Daryl performed a series of moves that worked together to place me flat on my back. The leverage was powerful.

When you invite Jesus into your life, the King of Kings adopts you. When you need to wrestle against invisible forces, he coaches you. Think of it this way. God has a prayer strategy for your life and those you are fighting for in prayer. As you listen for his voice, he teaches you how to pray with tremendous leverage.

Over the next few years, I would go months without prompting to pray for Tom. Then as I asked Jesus who was on his heart, he would remind me to wrestle in prayer for Tom. There were tournaments where Tom did not play well, yet I would spend hours praying for him. In 1993, I wrestled in prayer as Tom played in the Masters for the first time and finished in 3rd place. In 1994, I set aside a specific time to pray during the Memorial Tournament. Tom's score of twenty under par shattered the tournament record as he won by five shots. Tom Lehman's win at the Memorial was his first PGA victory. After the tournament, Jack Nicklaus said, "Bobby Jones once said at Augusta that I played a game with which he was not familiar. Well, this week, Tom Lehman played a game with which I am not familiar."

As I prayed for Tom, an interesting thing began to happen. I began to hear the voice of the Holy Spirit with a clarity that I had never experienced before. During the 1996 British Open, the Holy Spirit was so specific. I knew when to pray about alignment or grip pressure. I knew when to bind the spirit of fear or discouragement and how to pray specific scriptures at precise times. Early in the third round, I sensed a tremendous breakthrough in the spirit. I could sense people around the world interceding for Tom. During this round, I went from wrestling to rejoicing. I sensed that the spiritual forces opposing Tom were on the run.

The next day Tom rolled in the last putt and stood on the 18th green with his arms around his dad. In 1997 Tom became the number-one-rated golfer in the world. In the years that followed, millions of people heard the good news of the gospel.

Someone in your family or workplace is battling invisible forces and needs you to wrestle in prayer for them. As you ask God who is on his heart, he will show you. He will teach you to pray and to hear his voice. In my case, I was instructed not to reach out to Tom during my years of intercession and ask how I could pray. The Holy Spirit wanted me to rely entirely on him. He wanted me to know his voice.

In the Twin Cities, Search Ministries hosts events designed for seekers to encounter Jesus. I have attended their events and brought members of the Twins to share their faith. I asked the founder Jeff Siemon if a speaker or moment stood out across the years. There was no hesitation. Jeff told me about when Tom Lehman came and shared his testimony. He said that this message had changed countless lives and then gave me a recording of Tom's message.

I listened as Tom shared his memories of winning tournaments and playing in the Ryder cup as I drove away. Tom shared that he secretly felt like a failure despite the success and the speaking opportunities. One day in front of a mirror, all he saw was a hypocrite. He saw a man trying to earn the love of God, but who instead was a disappointment to him. Then he shared about a revelation of the love of Jesus that changed his life.

As Tom shared about being a disappointment to God, something broke inside me. Tom was saying what I had been afraid to admit to anyone. I was a hypocrite. I was a disappointment to God. Then Tom shared the unconditional love of Jesus.

I sat in a parking lot in stunned silence. As the love of God enveloped me, something marvelous occurred to me.

Jesus had asked me to wrestle for the one who would one day set me free.

REFLECT:

Who is Jesus asking me to intercede for?

What does Jesus desire to do through their life?

EQUIP:

How do you look for one who needs an intercessor?

BEGIN WITH WORSHIP: Before asking anything, begin by worshipping Jesus. Declare his greatness. As Andrew Murray shares, "Each time before you intercede, be quiet first, and worship God in His glory. Think of what He can do, and how He delights to hear the prayers of His redeemed people. Expect great things!"

As you are still before the Lord, take the limits off of God and begin with a blank piece of paper.

PRAY GOD'S WORD: Because God's Word is alive, ask the Holy Spirit to show you specific verses that exert tremendous leverage over this life. As you pray the very words of God, "The voice of the Lord echoes above the sea. The God of glory thunders. The Lord thunders over the mighty sea" (Psalm 29:3). As Anne Graham Lotz frequently says, "When you pray God's Word, you reverse the thunder." She also asks a probing question: "Who would be saved if you cared enough to pray?"

PARTNER WITH JESUS: When you don't know what to pray, picture the person standing before Jesus. In the very presence of Jesus, what is his heart for them? When you grow weary in prayer, remember that Jesus intercedes for you. "Therefore he is able, once and forever, to save those who come to God through him. He lives forever to intercede with God on their behalf" (Hebrews 7:25).

LET'S PRAY:

Father, I ask that you would teach me to pray. Coach me on how to pray your Word with tremendous leverage and to engage in spiritual warfare. You know my daily needs, but I dedicate my most significant efforts in prayer to the things that matter most to you. Show me who is on your heart. Hallowed be your name. Your kingdom come, your will be done, on earth as it is in heaven.

DISCUSS:

What is the difference between personal prayer and intercession?

Why does Jesus intercede for us?

"Who is to condemn? Christ Jesus is the one who died— more than that, who was raised—who is at the right hand of God, who indeed is interceding for us" (Romans 8:34).

Why does Jesus prompt us to intercede for an unsaved person?

"I will give him the honors of a victorious soldier, because he exposed himself to death. He was counted among the rebels. He bore the sins of many and interceded for rebels" (Isaiah 53:12).

How do we partner with the Holy Spirit in prayer?

"And the Holy Spirit helps us in our weakness. For example, we don't know what God wants us to pray for. But the Holy Spirit prays for us with groanings that cannot be expressed in words" (Romans 8:26).

If God is sovereign, how do our prayers release his work worldwide?

How do we pray for those in authority?

"I urge you, first of all, to pray for all people. Ask God to help them; intercede on their behalf, and give thanks for them. Pray this way for kings and all who are in authority so that we can live peaceful and quiet lives marked by godliness and dignity. This is good and pleases God our Savior, who wants everyone to be saved and to understand the truth" (1 Timothy 2:1-4).

What Scriptures are you praying over your family?

How do I become more like Jesus as I intercede?

20

Looking For The One
WHO FEELS ABANDONED

*"Jesus was forsaken of the Father that
we might never be forsaken."*

Warren Wiersbe

WHEN OUR SON Kyle was 13 years old, he was injured in a car accident. The emergency room doctor told us that Kyle had lost circulation to the lower portion of his left leg, so they immediately ordered an air ambulance. The good news? The surgeon was able to replace the crushed vein with a Goretex vein and restore circulation. The bad news? The surgeon told us that the car's bumper had crushed the nerves above Kyle's knee and that he might not walk normally again.

If you have spent a sleepless night in a hospital room, you can relate to what Sherrie and I went through. The next day, the doctor confirmed that he had no feeling from his knee to his foot. As I looked down at Kyle, I thought about his love of golf. He was always on the move, and now I pictured him spending the rest of his life with a limp. My heart was crushed with grief and loss, and I was too weary to pray. I felt abandoned.

I heard a familiar voice and looked up to see our dear friends Jim and Pam, who had just driven two hours to pray for Kyle. Given the circumstances and the long drive, you might think that Jim's prayer would be loud and long. But Jim's prayer for healing was like a gentle wind. As Jim said, "Amen," Kyle said, "I can feel something in my leg. It's like an electric current." I placed my hand on Kyle's foot and immediately felt this "electricity" pulsating every few seconds. With her finger, Sherrie drew a circle on the bottom of Kyle's foot.

There are moments in the presence of God that we never forget. Church services with thousands of worshippers or a verse coming alive to us from the pages of Scripture. But what of the moment when you go from feeling alone and abandoned to being touched by Jesus? At this moment, Kyle quietly said, "You're drawing a circle on the bottom of my foot." The next day Kyle was walking down the hallway, and our doctor shook his head as he said, "I don't use the word miracle very often. But I saw the damage firsthand. I saw the crushed nerves. This is a miracle!"

That night Kyle and I were talking about Jim's prayer and what Jesus had done for Kyle that afternoon. It was like a dream! I said goodnight, and as I was leaving the room, the Holy Spirit whispered, "Go tell David who I am."

David was the patient in the next room, and we had discovered from one of the nurses that he had been in a coma for several weeks. The nurse summarized his condition: "David was injured in a four-wheeler accident, and because of the abdominal infection, his upper and lower G.I. tract had to be disconnected. He's lost half of his body weight, and his blood is septic. Medically there is no hope."

On any other day, I suppose I might have hesitated to walk into a hospital room to speak to someone in a coma. But this was not any other day. When I entered the room, the blizzard of tubes and monitors was overwhelming. I saw the airbags around David's legs. Then I met David's girlfriend, Jeanne. We had noticed her standing by his bedside, and the nurses shared that she came almost every day and would stand by David for hours. Because our rooms were close together, there were times when we could hear her voice, "David, don't give up. Don't give up." I asked Jeanne if I could pray for David, and when she agreed, I closed my eyes. The moment my eyes closed, I "saw" David. He was alone in the woods, and from the expression on his face, he was lost. He felt abandoned.

As I opened my eyes, I said, "David, before I pray, I want you to know something. I see you standing in the woods, feeling lost and alone. You feel abandoned. But God has not abandoned you. He is right here and sent his son Jesus to give his life for you. He loves you, and He has a name. 'Holy, holy, holy, is the Lord God Almighty, who was and is and is to come' (Revelation 4:8, ESV)."

When I said, "Holy, holy, holy," David flinched. It was almost imperceptible, but I saw his arms move. Then in the corners of David's eyes, it looked like tears were beginning to form.

"David—God wants you to know who he is. He is holy, holy, holy." This time there was no mistake; David's arms moved again. I repeated Revelation 4:8 over and over, and each time David's body responded. A few minutes later, when I spoke, "He is holy, holy, holy," the healing power of God was released. The closest thing I can compare it to is the body's reaction to heart defib paddles. It was like a shock wave. David's entire body pulsated and stiffened from the power of God.

"David, I believe that Jesus is awakening you because he wants you to invite him in." I briefly shared the gospel and said, "If you would like to invite Jesus to be your savior, to forgive every sin, just squeeze Jeanne's hand." Jeanne sobbed, "He won't...stop...squeezing... my hand."

"David, Jesus hears the cry of your heart. You are forgiven and set free by the one who is holy, holy, holy—the Lord God Almighty!"

Then something went through my mind. "Wouldn't it be something if David opened his eyes?" At that moment, David's eyes opened. He looked at me, and then he looked at Jeanne. As I watched their faces, I thought about the look on the face of Jesus when he watches one of us come to life. He created us to know him. He gave us life to receive his abundant life.

Suddenly David began to claw at the restraints and airbags. He was trying to get out of bed! At that moment, the night nurse swept away the curtain and asked, "What is going on in here?!" As she glared at me, she announced that David's pulse had just doubled. "You need to get out of here!" In the hallway, Jeanne shared that she had been praying day after day that somehow David would regain consciousness and have one more chance to give his life to Christ. She shared that David spent days alone in the woods and about the day of his four-wheeler accident.

When I arrived the next day, I was devastated to see David once again unresponsive in his bed. It looked like he had fallen back into a coma. I asked his nurse for an update, and her eyes lit up. "He's not in a coma. He won't stop trying to get out of bed. We finally had to sedate him!" A few minutes later, an older woman with jet-black hair came down the hallway holding a large book. She asked, "Are you the man from last night?" After a word of greeting, she held up an old family Bible and said, "I've come here to read this book to my son." She walked into David's room, placed the Bible on the tray over his bed, and turned to the first page. Then in a determined voice she began to read. "In the beginning, God created the heaven and the earth" (Genesis 1:1, KJV).

I followed David's progress on Caring Bridge. Within a few days, he was standing by his bed. A few days later, he walked down the hallway. Several weeks later, the doctors went in to reconnect his digestive system. The family shared that after the surgery, a doctor at Mayo Clinic told them that no one had ever recovered from this condition. No one had recovered until David.

When I reflect on David's healing, I think of the God who desires to reveal his glory. I remember these words from Dane Ortlund. "Christ was sent not to mend wounded people or wake sleepy people or advise confused people or inspire bored people or spur on lazy people or educate ignorant people, but to raise dead people" (from *Gentle and Lowly*).

Years later, I am walking down a fairway, and a young man is walking beside me. There is no trace of a limp. As I look at Kyle, I think about the day that Jesus healed our son and opened David's eyes. "Holy, holy, holy is the Lord God Almighty!"

REFLECT:

Who do I know that feels abandoned?

Have I ever felt abandoned?

EQUIP:

How do I look for the one who feels abandoned?

REMEMBER: Begin by remembering the times you have lost hope. As you remember, God is making room in your heart for someone's heartache. He is releasing compassion through you.

RELATE: You can assure them that even the greatest followers of God have felt abandoned. Even a king named David:

> "Do not abandon me, O Lord.
> Do not stand at a distance, my God.

Come quickly to help me,
O Lord my savior" (Psalm 38:21-22).

As David was lying in bed after his accident, we can imagine why he felt abandoned by God. But this feeling is not reserved for hospital rooms. People all around you are losing hope. The finances are not enough, or the healing never came. The dream of holding a baby is gone.

THE CROSS OF CHRIST: As you look for this one, there are many things you can do for them. You can set aside time to listen to their heart. You can help them financially or serve them in practical ways. You can walk with them. You can hold them. But when you guide them to the cross of Christ, they begin to experience his presence. They experience supernatural compassion because Jesus ministers to their pain in ways that we cannot. As you gently bring them to the cross of Christ, you declare something life-changing. Again: "Jesus was forsaken of the Father that we might never be forsaken" (Warren Wiersbe).

SONS AND DAUGHTERS: I recently read something that broke my heart. "No one cared that he died without descendants" (Isaiah 53:8). As I thought about our children and grandchildren, I saw a new facet of the sacrifice of Jesus. Then verse 10 seemed to jump from the page. "Yet when his life is made an offering for sin, he will have many descendants" (Isaiah 53:10). As a follower of Jesus you are his descendant, and as you look for the one who feels abandoned, you are bringing a son or daughter to Jesus.

LET'S PRAY:

Lord Jesus, there is someone who feels abandoned because they believe you abandoned them. Before I walk into their life, please walk into my life. Show me any place in my heart that needs to be healed. Do not stand at a distance, my God.

Now, open my eyes to the one who feels abandoned by you. Give me your compassion and help me walk into their life with a declaration of who you are. Teach me how to love them and care for them as I declare your word to them. "The Lord will not reject his people; he will not abandon his special possession" (Psalm 94:14).

As I stretch out my hand, may there be a release of the power of God. "Stretch out your hand with healing power; may miraculous signs and wonders be done through the name of your holy servant Jesus" (Acts 4:30).

As I look for this one, make me more like Jesus.

DISCUSS:

Is there a time you have felt abandoned by God?

When we feel abandoned, why does Jesus know how we feel?

"At this point many of his disciples turned away and deserted him" (John 6:66).

"My God, my God, why have you abandoned me?" (Matthew 27:46)

Why did King David feel abandoned by God?

"My God, my God, why have you abandoned me? Why are you so far away when I groan for help? Every day I call to you, my God, but you do not answer. Every night you hear my voice, but I find no relief" (Psalm 22:1-2).

What do you think inspired these words from Saint Augustine: "God always pours His grace into empty hands"?

How do we know that God has not abandoned us?

"'To whom will you compare me? Who is my equal?' asks the Holy One. 'Look up into the heavens. Who created all the stars?' He brings them out like an army, one after another, calling each by its name. Because of his great power and incomparable strength, not a single one is missing. O Jacob, how can you say the Lord does not see your troubles? O Israel, how can you say God ignores your rights? Have

you never heard? Have you never understood? The Lord is the everlasting God, the Creator of all the earth. He never grows weak or weary. No one can measure the depths of his understanding. He gives power to the weak and strength to the powerless. Even youths will become weak and tired, and young men will fall in exhaustion. But those who trust in the Lord will find new strength. They will soar high on wings like eagles. They will run and not grow weary. They will walk and not faint" (Isaiah 40:25-31).

"For the mountains may move and the hills disappear, but even then my faithful love for you will remain" (Isaiah 54:10).

When sharing Jesus, how do you see the power of God?

"For when we brought you the Good News, it was not only with words but also with power, for the Holy Spirit gave you full assurance that what we said was true" (1 Thessalonians 1:5).

As I look for the one who feels abandoned, how do I become more like Jesus?

Looking For The One

DESPERATE TO REACH HER FRIENDS

"They saw that God had given me the responsibility of preaching the gospel...."

Galatians 2:7

WHEN I ENJOY JESUS he guides me to lost people. In other words, when I am taking a walk and singing worship songs, I find myself in a God story. On the other hand, when I am walking around trying to find lost people, I seem to succeed less.

A few years ago, I stayed in downtown Chicago and, for my morning workout, decided to walk north around Lake Michigan. It was a glorious morning, and I had the walkway to myself. As I took in the scenery, I began to sing.

Suddenly a voice was calling to me. "Can you help us? Our team needs a picture taken." I looked up a path that led to a park, and a young lady was smiling down at me. When I arrived at the park, I was introduced to a college volleyball team.

As the girls lined up for their picture, I mentioned my history as a wedding photographer and asked if they would mind moving a few feet to be in better light. Within moments we had a fantastic picture to capture the moment. I asked two or three girls about their season, their coach, and what it was like to balance academics with all of the practice and travel for matches. I noticed that the entire team had gathered around and was listening intently.

Then the whisper of the Holy Spirit. "Tell them about Jesus."

"I am so honored to serve as your official photographer, and I hope you have a great season, but if you have just a few minutes, I would like to share something with you. I am part of a ministry called Baseball Chapel, and I serve the Minnesota Twins. That's why I am in Chicago this weekend. I don't know about you, but in baseball, I've met a bunch of guys who have heard of God, but to be honest, they don't know him personally. It's Christmas or Easter services or a list of rules but no real relationship with God.

"Would any of you like to know how to have your own relationship with Jesus?"

We believe that the people around us are not interested in the gospel or even hostile to a God conversation. I have found the opposite to be true. I have been amazed at the people going through life with no idea of who Jesus is. They are not antagonistic to the gospel; they have never heard the gospel.

I would have been delighted if two or three girls had stayed around to talk about Jesus. But it was not two or three. The entire team nodded, smiled, and said, "Yes!" Then they moved even closer to their new team photographer.

By the way, I feel compelled to share that this college volleyball team was headed to the beach for the day and dressed for the occasion. In other words, twenty young ladies in swimsuits stepped toward me in unison.

Purity is vital to our spiritual growth and even our protection. If our motives are impure, we turn people off. If our eyes are impure, we push people away. But purity is also at the center of sharing the good news of Jesus. "He alone examines the motives of our hearts" (1 Thessalonians 2:4).

At this moment, all I saw were the eyes of young ladies who wanted to know Jesus.

I walked the team through a chapel message that I had recently shared with the Twins called "The Backpack." (My friend and gifted counselor Todd Monger inspired this concept.) I asked them to imagine playing volleyball with a backpack filled with rocks.

"Can you play volleyball that way?"

"Yes."

"Can you play as well?"

"No!"

"As you stand on the court, there are many 'rocks' that you can place in your backpack. Fear of losing your scholarship. Fear of failure. Knowing that you are not at 100% because of an injury. A teammate looking at you with anger or jealousy, or a coach you can never please. A mom or dad that points out your mistakes. The longer you play, the heavier the backpack." As they nodded, I saw the pain on their faces.

"So, how do you remove the rocks from your backpack?

"You can tell yourself not to worry about the coach or your parents, but that doesn't work. You still carry around the pain and the pressure. The only way to unpack your backpack is to take out the biggest rock. It's twice as big as the others, and if you don't remove this one rock, you can't remove any of the other rocks.

"Any idea what the big rock is?" The girls gave their best guesses. Words like fear and guilt came flying out.

I paused to let the suspense build, and then I shared that the big rock is identity. "Is your identity limited to your performance as an athlete, or are you far more valuable? Because if you are only a volleyball player, you carry all of the rocks that go along with a life of performance. But the good news is that God did not create you to be a performer. God sent his son Jesus to die for you so you could belong to him. To be identified as his adopted son or daughter. To stop performing and be accepted by him. To be completely forgiven.

"The death of Jesus on the cross was for you, and the moment you receive him as your savior, you belong to him. Now you can play volleyball with all of your focus and passion, knowing that failure can't steal your identity. If you fail at volleyball, you still have unfailing love."

I prayed a blessing over the girls and gave them a moment to invite Jesus into their life. As I walked down the path back to Lake Michigan, my heart was singing. Then a voice behind me. "Dave— wait!" I looked around as a member of the team came running down the path.

"You have no idea! I prayed last night that God would send someone to share the gospel with my teammates. I prayed because I felt desperate. I have tried to share my faith, but I can't get through. I asked Jesus to send someone. And the moment you began to speak, I recognized your voice. I'm from the Twin Cities. Our family listens to PraiseLive! I think it's amazing that God answered my prayer so quickly and, on top of that, sent someone whose voice I already knew. Thank you!"

This time as I walked along Lake Michigan, I sensed Jesus singing over me!

REFLECT:

Do I enjoy Jesus?

EQUIP:

How do I look for the one desperate to reach her friends?

WALK WITH JESUS: The next time you go on a walk, sing to Jesus! As you delight in his presence, you might hear someone calling for help. Be open because someone is ready to meet Jesus.

KEEP IT SIMPLE: The backpack is not the most profound message I have shared. But I don't know of a message that has changed more lives. Dare to share Jesus in personal creative ways! Think in advance of stories, illustrations, or visuals that can open hearts to the good news.

PURE HEART/PURE MOTIVES: My friend Bob Hoskins of OneHope changed my life with this challenge. Instead of focusing on the number of people you are reaching, ask Jesus for a pure heart and pure motives.

REACH THE ONE: As you look for the one you are engaged in supernatural multiplication. But these are not just numbers, the one you reach is crying out for their friends. "Peter and John won the crippled beggar, and his transformed life led to the conversion of two thousand people! Like Jesus, the apostles took time for individuals" (Warren Wiersbe).

LET'S PRAY:

Jesus—I worship you this day. I praise your name! As I enjoy you and abide with you, I know that you will cause me to be fruitful. Purify my heart and eyes so that I don't hinder what you want to do through my life. Give me stories and illustrations that help people understand who you are. Thank you for loving and adopting me. Belonging to you changes everything! Thank you for removing my backpack filled with sin and shame.

DISCUSS:

As you go through life, what is in your backpack?

What does it mean to delight yourself in the Lord?

What are some of the benefits of purity?

"In a wealthy home some utensils are made of gold and silver, and some are made of wood and clay. The expensive utensils are used for special occasions, and the cheap ones are for everyday use. If you keep yourself pure, you will be a special utensil for honorable use. Your life will be clean, and you will be ready for the Master to use you for every good work" (2 Timothy 2:20-21).

What does it mean to be responsible for preaching the gospel?

"They saw that God had given me the responsibility of preaching the gospel..." (Galatians 2:7).

As I help someone reach their friends, how do I become more like Jesus?

Looking For The One
WAITING FOR THE GOOD NEWS

"What matters most to me is to finish what God started: the job the Master Jesus gave me of letting everyone I meet know all about this incredibly extravagant generosity of God."

Acts 20:24, The Message

IT WAS MIDNIGHT, and the pain was excruciating. For a moment, I thought it was just a stomachache, and then I doubled over. To make matters worse, I was in a hotel room in Houston, Texas, over 1,000 miles from home.

I took a cab to a clinic that the hotel said was open all night, and on the way, the pain intensified. Now I was on my hands and knees, crawling toward the clinic's front door. Drenched in sweat, I inched my way toward the front desk. As I looked up, a woman stared down and began to scold me. She thought I was under the influence of something. She pointed to the door, "If you don't have insurance, you need to leave."

Moments later, I heard the words "perforated ulcer" and found myself in an ambulance on the way to a Houston hospital. After surgery, the pain level the next day was unbearable. The tiniest movement reminded me that I had a 5" scar on my abdominal wall.

At this moment, two nurses arrived and very sweetly told me that I would get up and walk down the hallway. Somehow I managed a few shuffling steps.

The next day I looked up and nearly burst into tears. Sherrie walked in the door with my dear friends Jesse and Becky Crain. Sherrie is the love of my life, but she is also a former nurse and a lifetime student of health and nutrition. Within moments I was gulping down a variety of supplements.

On my next attempt to walk down the hallway, I could still barely stand when a man walked up and asked if he could pray for me. This stranger began to pray, and the power of God began to flow. I felt a wave of heat and electricity that went from my head to my feet. He prayed for healing, and then he prayed for my life to touch the nations. He told me that God has a special and unique work for me and that the time was now. I began to cry.

Moments later, Dorgival shared his story of growing up with no knowledge of God. He reached a crisis point when a tumor protruded from his abdominal area, and he had no hope of recovery. But one day, a follower of Jesus came and prayed for his healing. Jesus completely healed Dorgival! His face lit up as he shared, "That is why I come to this hospital to pray for the sick one day a week."

Dorgival told me that if the pain returns at night, to declare Psalm 103:

> Bless the Lord, O my soul,
> and all that is within me,
> bless his holy name!
> Bless the Lord, O my soul,
> and forget not all his benefits,
> who forgives all your iniquity,
> who heals all your diseases
> (Psalm 103:1-3, ESV).

That night the pain was so intense that I was unable to sleep. As I began to speak the words of Psalm 103, my abdominal area began to grow warm. Then the warmth intensified until it felt like a furnace. Several times in the next half hour, I reached for the call button, fearing something might be wrong.

From that moment, the presence of God saturated my room. When the nurses would ask if I wanted to watch TV, the answer was no. Several visitors and even members of the hospital staff commented on the unusual presence in my room.

On my next walk down the hallway, it was so odd to hear the sounds of television coming from each room that I walked by. In one room, the sound of an old western. In the next room, the sound of a political talk show. In the next room, something that sounded sexually suggestive. A few steps down the hallway, I heard someone cursing. When I returned to my room, the Holy Spirit gently asked a question. "Which room do you want to be in?"

I was speechless, but the message was clear. You can choose to be in any of the other rooms, or you can choose to be in this room with the manifest presence of God.

My friend Rob Hoskins of OneHope frequently shares his passion for a pure heart and pure motives. Rob testifies that God can provide any financial resource or staff persons, but what he looks for are pure hearts and pure motives. I asked Jesus to take me on a guided tour of my heart and show me any room in my heart that needed repentance.

When I was cleared to fly home to Minnesota, a nurse named Maria introduced herself. "You need to know that you are the talk of the floor. No one has ever recovered this quickly from this surgery." Maria looked around the room, "The nurses have told me that there is a presence in this room."

I shared with Maria that the presence in the room was Jesus and asked if she would like to know him. I watched the wonder in her eyes as she shared what her mother told her when she was leaving for America. "Maria, someday someone will tell you how to know Jesus. Maria, when that day comes, you must give yourself to him."

What followed was one of the most beautiful moments I have ever witnessed. Maria heard that Jesus had given his life for her sins and that she could invite him to be her Savior. She was smiling and crying at the same time. She had spent years wondering how to know Jesus, and now it was like watching someone who had crossed a desert take an unlimited drink of cold water.

As Maria left my room, the Holy Spirit whispered again, "Which room do you want to be in?"

REFLECT:

Which room do I want to be in?

EQUIP:

How do I look for the one waiting for the good news?

AROMA OF JESUS: Reflect for a moment on the programs and media that are a part of your life. Is there content that is grieving the person of the Holy Spirit? Ask Jesus to take you on a guided tour of your heart. As you surrender to a pure heart and pure motives, be ready for people all around you to be drawn to the aroma of Jesus. "It is in His presence and through His grace that whatever of fragrance or beauty may be found in us comes forth" (Hudson Taylor, *Union and Communion*).

WALK WITH JESUS: To see the lost, lonely, and broken through the eyes of Jesus, we need to walk with Jesus. This is why Jesus invited his apostles into a relationship before sending them out to preach. "He appointed twelve that they might be with him and that he might send them out to preach" (Mark 3:14).

FAMILY MATTERS: My heart is unmoved if I think of the lost as a faraway statistic. When I understand that the one waiting for good news is my brother or sister, I am compelled to reach them. Jesus calls Maria his sister, which means that she is my sister. "So now Jesus and the ones he makes holy have the same Father. That is why Jesus is not ashamed to call them his brothers and sisters" (Hebrews 2:11).

LET'S PRAY:

Jesus, as I walk along, there are so many rooms demanding my time and attention, but my heart belongs to you. I surrender what I see and hear, and I ask that you grant me a pure heart and pure motives. "Point out anything in me that offends you, and lead me along the path of everlasting life" (Psalm 139:24). I am willing to go looking for the one, but I pray that you bring them to me today.

DISCUSS:

How does prayer fuel the spread of the gospel?

"Finally, dear brothers and sisters, we ask you to pray for us. Pray that the Lord's message will spread rapidly and be honored wherever it goes, just as when it came to you" (2 Thessalonians 3:1).

How are we empowered to share the good news?

"For God has not given us a spirit of fear and timidity, but of power, love, and self-discipline. So never be ashamed to tell others about our Lord" (2 Timothy 1:7-8).

Who is waiting to hear the good news from you?

"My ambition has always been to preach the Good News where the name of Christ has never been heard, rather than where a church has already been started by someone else. I have been following the plan spoken of in the Scriptures, where it says, 'Those who have never been told about him will see, and those who have never heard of him will understand'" (Romans 15:20-21).

As I look for the one waiting for the good news, how do I become more like Jesus?

Looking For The One
CALLED BY NAME

*"I praise You, Lord, for the incredible value You place on
sinners! You do not passively wait for us to come to You.
You actively, passionately seek us out of our wanderings
and hiding places. Your pursuit is relentless. Nine out
of ten is not good enough for You. 99 out of 100 is still
unacceptable. You are not willing that any should perish."*

NIV Worship Bible

I ONLY HAD A FEW minutes, and I could feel the tension building
as I waited. I had been trying to solve a computer glitch for several
days and had spent hours trying to resolve the issue. A young man
approached as I thought about all of the wasted time.

As John began to help me, I scolded myself for not coming in
earlier. He was talking to himself and typing at high speed. Then he
brought in a co-worker who helps him process the replacement of
defective software. As we waited for the computer to download the
update, I asked a question.

"Is there a story behind your name?"

John looked at me cautiously, and our eyes locked for several
seconds. John glanced around and then began to share about growing up in the Middle East. As he shared about his family, he glanced

around again. Now he told me that there were several times when his life was spared. "There were so many times when I should have been dead."

In the silence, I felt prompted to gently ask again, "Is there a story behind your name?"

John had a faraway look in his eyes, and then he said, "My aunt thought it would be a good idea to name me after someone in the Bible." He quickly added, "But I'm not religious."

John was surprised to find out that one of the followers of Jesus was named John. I shared one of the things that John had written about Jesus. "For God so loved the world, that he gave his only Son, that whoever believes in him should not perish but have eternal life" (John 3:16, ESV).

The first line of The Salvation Poem is, "Jesus, you died upon a cross." As I shared with John why Jesus had gone to the cross, I noticed two things. John's eyes were filling with light, and no one was coming near us. It was like an invisible shield had been placed around our conversation.

When I asked John if he would like to be forgiven of every sin and give his life to Jesus, there was no hesitation. The man who had no interest in religion moments ago was ready to follow Jesus.

I handed The Salvation Poem card to John, and he read these words:

Jesus, you died upon a cross
And rose again to save the lost
Forgive me now of all my sin
Come by my Savior, Lord, and Friend

As John said, "Friend," he looked at me and then looked up. Then he raised his hands and repeatedly said, "Something is happening to me!" When John's eyes returned to my eyes, they were filled with joy.

I walked John through the last two lines of the poem and the amazing truth that Jesus was now living within him and that Jesus is the one who begins to change our life.

Change my life and make it new
And help me, Lord, to live for you

As John took out his phone and began to show me pictures of his hometown and his family, the software download was complete. As corrupt software was replaced, John's old life was replaced with new life in Christ.

As I walked out, I gave thanks for an aunt who spoke a name so that her nephew would be called by name.

A few days later, I stopped by the store to follow up on John, and a young lady informed me that he was not working. She asked if there was anything she could do to help me, and I shared that I was stopping by to see how John was doing. Now it was her turn to ask a question.

"What do you do?"

"People all around us have heard of God, but they don't know him. I work at a ministry called PraiseLive, and our programming is designed so that you can experience Jesus. We want you to have your own relationship with him." Without any suggestion from me, she immediately opened her phone and downloaded our app. Then she linked the phone to a speaker in the store and hit the play button.

The song "His Name" from Urban Rescue was beginning to play, and these words filled the store:

There's a father when your father walks away
A friend when no one else knows your name

A light that shines when all the world goes dark
A hand that holds you when you fall apart
His name is Healer of your deepest scars
Father of your broken heart
His name is
Mercy
Power
Freedom
Oh, His name
Oh, His name
His name is Jesus

As the song played, she linked the music to other speakers in the store. Then, she picked up the speaker and held it in her arms.

As she heard the name of Jesus, she laid her head on the speaker, she began to whisper the name of Jesus.

REFLECT:

Is there a story behind your name?

EQUIP:

How do I look for the one who is called by name?

SPEAK A NAME: As Jesus ministers to people, over and over, he speaks their name. Saying a name is intimate, personal, and powerful. "But the Lord answered her, 'Martha, Martha, you are anxious and troubled about many things'" (Luke 10:41, ESV).

AUTHENTIC QUESTIONS: We've all asked questions that are not real. "How ya doing today?!" I was pumping fuel at Costco in Fort Myers, Florida, and noticed the attendant's nametag. When I asked Daniel if there was a story behind his name, he instantly shared being raised in a Christian family but having no relationship with Christ. Daniel gave his life to Jesus on the spot! Daniel needed to know that it was not too late and that God still saw him. Because of a question about his name, Daniel can join Hagar in declaring, "You are the God who sees me" (Genesis 16:13).

AVOID DISAPPROVAL: The young lady from the computer store did not commit to Christ. But she held a speaker as Jesus sang over her. I don't know why her heart was only open for a moment, but to pressure her for a decision would have been to associate the gospel with disapproval.

AMAZING GRACE: As I purchased groceries, the young lady behind the cash register was wearing a nametag that said "Grace." I asked her if there was a story behind such a beautiful name. "My mom could not have children for many years, and then she finally had me. She wanted to thank God for my life." She told me that the word grace is in the Bible someplace, "But I don't know where it is." What an amazing honor to share with her, "God saved you by his grace when you believed" (Ephesians 2:8).

LET'S PRAY:

Thank you for love that is so personal. As I hear you whisper my name, I am drawn to you because to hear my name is to hear your heart. Please anoint me to perceive when a name is about to open a door you are knocking on.

DISCUSS:

What does it mean to carry the name of Jesus?

"When I discovered your words, I devoured them. They are my joy and my heart's delight, for I bear your name, O Lord God of Heaven's Armies" (Jeremiah 15:16).

What does it mean to see God?

"Have I truly seen the One who sees me?" (Genesis 16:13)

Why does God care about my name?

"See, I have written your name on the palms of my hands" (Isaiah 49:16).

As I look for the one to call by name, how do I become more like Jesus?

Looking For The One
WHO NEEDS TO BE ENCOURAGED

"Flatter me, and I may not believe you. Criticize me, and I may not like you. Ignore me, and I may not forgive you. Encourage me, and I will not forget you."

William Arthur Ward

"HOW WOULD YOU LIKE to sell some soap?"

Dad's question hung in the air, but from the look on his face, I knew the answer was "Yes." When I was around 12 years old, Dad decided to train me in the fine art of door-to-door sales. Never mind that I had zero interest in selling Shaklee soap. Dad's eyes shone with the zeal of an evangelist as he pressed the bottles into my hands.

Instead of sending me down the street, Dad decided to instruct me in the fine art of sales. My first assignment was to knock on his front door. Dad skillfully played the part of a grumpy old-timer that I warmed up before making my pitch. After a few comments about the weather and the Vikings, I would launch into my presentation. There were times when the old-timer was polite and other times when he was mean. Dad would evaluate each sales call and gently point out where I had lost the sale.

Dad stressed over and over that the real art of sales is to know how to handle the client's objections. An effective salesperson sees an objection as an opportunity to discover what the client wants. He taught me how to detect confusion, and then he taught me how to ask for the sale. "David—if you don't ask for the sale, you won't get the sale. Now here is the key. After you ask for the sale, be quiet!" I only sold a few bottles of soap. But I did endear myself to several women who appreciated my demonstrations of how wonderfully the soap cleaned their kitchens. Of course, there were the little old ladies who invited me to stay for fresh cookies and ice cold milk.

Dad was passionate about sales because he sold dairy equipment and oversaw a sales network reaching five states. But the real reason Dad loved sales is that he loved to encourage people.

When I was 14 years old, Dad asked me to be his "wheelman." He was driving over 50,000 miles a year and was unconcerned that his wheelman did not have a license. I remember many dinners with salespeople on our road trips that had nothing to do with bulk tanks or milking machines but everything to do with encouragement. These men knew it was safe to open up about their marriage and family.

As I prepared to enter college, I saw that look on Dad's face again. There was a new energy-saving device for dairy farmers and an opportunity to buy the rights to half of the state of Minnesota. The only catch was that I would need to purchase thousands of dollars of inventory, tools, and a pickup truck. I would need to glue plastic water lines and solder copper pipes. My hands were shaking as I signed a banknote for $40,000. Then my Dad signed his name next to mine.

Once again, Dad coached me and warned me that I would hear "No" repeatedly. He was right. There was no interest or encouragement as I drove from farm to farm. The low point was a farm near Marshall, Minnesota, where I drove up as a dozen farmers were gathering around a hay rack. I made my presentation, and after a short silence, the owner said, "I don't want your new-fangled energy device. Now get back into your shiny new pickup and get the _____ off my farm." As I walked away, his friends roared in laughter.

Driving away, I knew that it was over. It would take years of minimum wages to pay off the loan, but I was sick of the rejection. As I turned onto the next gravel road, the Holy Spirit whispered something that changed my life. "It's not over. It's just beginning. Drive into the next farm."

The next driveway belonged to a young farmer who took one look at my new-fangled energy device and said, "Yes!" When his electrical bill went down a dollar a day, he began to tell his friends and neighbors. When I shared his story, I quickly signed up several salespeople to cover my half of Minnesota.

My $40,000 debt was paid in full, and one year of college tuition was funded. In addition, I was going to college with several salespeople selling my product. I even developed a lease program to have a steady income. As my friends made plans for the weekend, I would head out to spend time with my team and deliver orders in person. We would go on calls together, and I would encourage them. At dinner, they would open up about their marriage and family.

As God provided for my college education, he grew my faith and taught me business principles. But there was something else at stake. Thirty-five years later, a man at Costco needed help with his pots and pans.

One of the benefits of buying tires at Costco is free tire rotations. It takes about an hour to get your tires rotated, and it's a great time to respond to emails. But one day, the Holy Spirit whispered that it was time to take a walk. Someone in the store was on his heart.

As I walked around the store, I noticed a display set up for a young man selling pots and pans. I was in immediate sticker shock.

These were costly pots and pans. I stood in the back of the crowd and listened carefully to his presentation. There was a good-sized crowd, but they were restless. No one made a purchase or stayed around to ask questions.

As the crowd walked away, I asked how things were going and heard the story of a young man who was discouraged. He had been traveling for several months and was weary of the road. Then he opened up about the lack of sales and the growing financial pressure. He was thinking about quitting.

I shared several things about his presentation that I thought were effective. I noted his smile and enthusiasm. His knowledge of the various packages was evident. Then I asked if he was open to adjusting his presentation. To my surprise, he immediately said, "Yes!"

"Let me tell you where you lost me and where I think you lost the crowd. Instead of opening with a description of your pots and pans, let's try to engage the audience. How about opening with, 'Think for a moment about the pots and pans in your kitchen. If you are like me, you have a lot of pots and pans, but only a few you count on. These pans cook evenly and last forever. The surface doesn't peel off when you scrape them. You don't break your wrist when you lift them from the stove. Then there are the pots and pans that wreck your meals and are worthless after a few years. You thought you were getting a good deal, but you were throwing your money away.'"

I told him that my first goal when I speak in churches or chapel services is to engage the audience. I focus on why a topic matters and don't move from that focus until I feel the room becoming quiet. If they don't understand the "why" in your talk, they won't engage in what you say. "Instead of focusing on your talk, focus on the people. Watch their faces. When you see them begin to nod or smile, it's time to share about a product that improves their life."

Finally, we discussed the close of his presentation. He had just presented five purchase options, and it was confusing with the charts and numbers. "For the next group, present one option. Keep it simple with something like, 'There are many ways to invest in these, but the one that I think makes the most sense is...'"

As a new crowd gathered, I slipped to the back and began to pray. The difference between the two presentations was remarkable. Instead of a rapid, memorized talk, this felt like a conversation among friends. He was more relaxed and more natural. He was making eye contact. As he explained why the pots and pans were a long-term investment in your health, the crowd began to focus. Instead of a sales pitch, this was a life coach who wanted the best for you. When the time was right, he walked them through making the purchase. Instead of several options, he shared one clearly defined plan that was the best value. Several people pressed forward to pick up brochures and asked questions. Then the moment of truth. Two ladies stepped up and purchased the sets he recommended. When they left, his face was radiant!

As the crowd slipped away, we shared a moment of celebration. Then I asked about his church background and quickly found out that he had attended a few services but had no interest in anything religious. I told him that I had been praying for him.

I silently prayed as I said, "A few minutes ago, we saw what happened as you developed a relationship and then explained why your pots and pans mattered. Jesus wants to develop a relationship with you. He wants you to know why you matter to him. He loves you!"

We talked about the sin that separates us from God, but the peace and purpose from a relationship with Jesus. We discussed why Jesus gave his life on the cross. From the look on his face, I sensed it was time to ask for the decision.

"Would you like to invite Jesus to be your Savior, Lord, and Friend?" There was no need to wait as he instantly said, "Yes!" He lifted a beautiful prayer of repentance and salvation. Not one person stopped at his booth to ask about pots and pans during this conversation. The King of Kings kept every distraction away.

We exchanged phone numbers, and on Saturday, Sherrie and I invited him to join us Sunday morning at church. Our new friend arrived a few minutes before the service, and we gave him a Life Application Bible. Then this man walking with Jesus for two days told us, "I now know what my purpose is. My calling is to be a pastor!"

As we said goodbye, I thought about how much I disliked selling soap and how hard it was to sell dairy equipment. Then I thought about the God who ordered the footsteps of a weary salesman so that the love of Jesus could find him.

How marvelous!

REFLECT:

What are the jobs or experiences in my life where I felt like a failure?

Is there someone in my life who is discouraged?

Does it feel like a sales pitch or the beginning of a relationship when I share the gospel?

EQUIP:

How do I look for the one that needs encouragement?

INVEST IN SUCCESS: A few years ago, I met a youth pastor who released encouragement with a powerful statement. "I want to be a part of your success." As you might imagine, his youth group was multiplying! When you look for the one, find someone weary or discouraged, and find a way to build their life. Be a part of their success.

KEEP IT SIMPLE: As these relationships develop, you can now ask questions about their spiritual background. Listen with the eyes of your heart and then share why Jesus matters so much to you. When it is time to invite them to commit their life to Jesus, share why Jesus died upon a cross. Share the principle of how our sin separates us from a holy God. You don't need a memorized speech. Keep the focus on Jesus and speak from the heart! "For Christ didn't send me to baptize, but to preach the Good News—and not with clever speech, for fear that the cross of Christ would lose its power" (1 Corinthians 1:17).

ASK FOR THEIR HEART: This may be out of your comfort zone, but you need to give the invitation to follow Jesus at some point. Ask for their heart! As Dad said, "If you don't ask for the sale, you won't get the sale." You will know when the time is right as you look into their eyes. When you give the invitation, be quiet! Make room for the conviction of the Holy Spirit.

If there are objections or questions, instead of being defensive, be excited. Someone is giving you an insight into what matters most to them. If the answer is "No," be steadfast. The rejection is for Jesus and not for you.

If the answer is "Yes," take a moment to invite them to pray with you. To confess with their mouth that Jesus is Lord! Keep several Bibles on hand that you can give to a new believer. Be a part of their success!

LET'S PRAY:

Jesus, I thank you for every part of my story. Especially the chapters where I felt like a failure. I ask that you give me supernatural favor as I engage with the lost and those about to give up. Please help me to create a road map for their success. Open the eyes of my heart to see their heart. Please give me the courage to invite people to follow you.

DISCUSS:

Is there a failure in your life that can encourage someone to not give up?

"This is a trustworthy saying, and everyone should accept it: 'Christ Jesus came into the world to save sinners'—and I am the worst of them all" (1 Timothy 1:15).

What part of your story can God use to release encouragement?

Why does God's Word tell us not to neglect living in community?

> *"And let us not neglect our meeting together, as some people do, but encourage one another, especially now that the day of his return is drawing near"* (Hebrews 10:25).

How do I become more like Jesus as I look for the one to encourage?

Looking For The One
WHO NEEDS TO KNOW THEIR PURPOSE

"The two most important days of your life are the day you were born and the day you find out why."

Mark Twain

"HAVE YOU EVER been to Africa?" My new friend Graham Power from Capetown posed the question. I immediately sensed it was finally time for my first trip. Of course, this was long overdue since our radio ministry had received a calling to minister in Africa over 20 years ago. In the past two years, God has graciously given us satellite coverage over the Middle East and almost all of Africa. Also, he blessed us with numerous FM radio stations as affiliates. We had waited nearly 20 years, but now we cover this strategic area with praise, prayer, and the Word of God.

I quickly began calculating the hours it would take to fly to Capetown. There was also another consideration. In February 2020, Covid-19 was starting to speed up its march worldwide. What if the virus escalated? What if I were to get sick in South Africa? At this moment, Graham quietly added, "By the way, I have an extra ticket for the Federer and Nadal tennis match in Capetown." Sold!

The flight to Amsterdam was without a spiritual encounter, but the Capetown flight was a different story. I shared Jesus with a woman who owns a hospice center in Amsterdam and walked her through how to invite Jesus into her life. Then I met a nurse from South Africa with a passion for natural and alternative medicine. One of our conversations in the back of the plane lasted almost an hour. As I shared about the hope of Jesus, several of the flight attendants listened intently. When the flight crew announced that everyone leaving the plane would have their temperature taken, I suddenly felt warm. Thankfully it was all in my head, and I arrived safe and sound.

The following day, Graham arranged for his friend Nurden to take me for a tour of Capetown. Our first stop was a market on the Indian Ocean, and as we walked to the ocean, we passed a young man playing guitar with a small jar for donations. As we walked by, I sensed the Holy Spirit say, "Not yet." It was a pure delight to step up to the ocean and realize I was standing on the southern tip of this amazing continent. I stood facing the north and prayed over the people and nations. As we walked away from the shoreline, I realized we were walking by the young man again. This time the Holy Spirit said, "Now."

I stood for several minutes and listened to this gifted musician pour out his heart. After the song, we talked about his music, and then I added my investment to his glass jar. I found out that Manfred was traveling on his own and in a season of looking for direction and purpose.

I asked Manfred if he was a Christian, and he said, "Yes."

"Have you ever invited Jesus into your life?"

Manfred said, "No, I've never done that."

I shared the good news of the gospel with Manfred, and before asking him to give his life to Christ, I felt prompted to speak to him about his life purpose. "Manfred, I believe that if you give your life to Christ, he will take your love of music and storytelling and place his hand of blessing on your life. I believe that your purpose is to sing from the heart and to point people to Jesus."

Manfred's eyes held so many questions, and then his eyes were clear and determined.

"Would you like to give your life and music to Jesus?" Manfred's face broke into a smile as he said, "Yes!"

I have noticed that when eternity hangs in the balance, there is a sudden quiet. As we began to pray, even the wind and the waves seemed to calm. The Holy Spirit shields these moments from any interference or distractions. As someone steps from darkness into the light, you sense the attention of heaven.

Manfred prayed a beautiful prayer of repentance. When he began to play his guitar, it was a new song about Jesus. How wonderful! He stepped immediately into his calling and purpose!

I asked Manfred if he would like to share his testimony in a video, and he said, "I just gave my life to Jesus, and I believe in him dying on the cross for me. My music, my talents, and my gifts, I give it all to God. I surrender myself to Jesus. I believe in Jesus!"

The first person I reached out to in Africa received a revelation of his purpose and then a revelation of his Savior.

People all around us long to know their purpose and enter a relationship with their Creator. Sherrie and I recently met with a businessman helping us process something for our home. Because of Covid-19, the door to this conference room stood open with several staff persons within hearing distance. As I complimented Uriah about his name, he shared that his father was a pastor who named him after the man who lost his life in David and Bathsheba's story. "It was tough going through junior high school with a name like Uriah. Kids can be cruel."

Sherrie looked at Uriah, "Actually, I think of a man who refused to compromise on his principles when I think of Uriah. When the king offered him a night with his wife, he refused. When the king ordered him into harm's way, he obeyed orders."

Uriah quietly said, "No one has ever shared that perspective with me." We talked about David's prayer as he repented of his sin with Uriah and Bathsheba. You hear the brokenness of David as he prays, "Against you, and you alone, have I sinned; I have done what is evil in your sight" (Psalm 51:4).

As the conversation shifted to current events and Uriah's thoughts on our nation's future and economy, a phrase came to me repeatedly. "Uriah's calling is to be a storm chaser." I hesitated to speak this over Uriah, but the words came to me repeatedly.

I took a deep breath. "Uriah, I believe that your interest in the direction of our society and economy is because you will warn people all around you that a storm is coming. I think that God has called you to be a storm chaser. Someone who gets close enough to storms to understand them and then warn people to stay away from them."

The room became very still as Uriah showed us his forearms. He said, "I have goosebumps." Uriah was receiving a revelation of purpose and a revelation of Jesus at the same time.

When looking for the one, there are times when you invite a Manfred to commit his life to Jesus. You sense in your heart that it is time for a new life. There are other times with a Uriah when you plant a seed. As you may have noticed, Jesus did both. Some of the disciples walked with him for several months before they were ready to leave their nets and follow him. Jesus knew that sometimes questions have to be answered and relationships developed. He also knew exactly when to ask for a commitment to follow him.

We ask for a revelation of purpose that leads to a revelation of Jesus.

REFLECT:

Do I know my purpose?

How do I help someone find their purpose?

EQUIP:

How do I look for the one who needs to know their purpose?

FOCUS ON FOLLOWING: When you look for the one, it is not enough to ask if they are a Christian. People all around us say they are Christians but have no idea what it means to follow Jesus. People need to know that to follow Jesus is to follow him into our purpose. When Jesus saw Peter and Andrew throwing their nets into the water, he called out to them, "'Come, follow me, and I will show you how to fish for people!' And they left their nets at once and followed him" (Matthew 4:19-20). Peter and Andrew left their nets and stepped into their purpose.

RELEASE GOD'S WORD: As you sense God's heart for someone, and he begins to reveal their purpose, speak God's Word into them. "Do you have the gift of speaking? Then speak as though God himself were speaking through you" (1 Peter 4:11).

PURPOSE STATEMENTS: Several years ago my friend Byron and I met with a well-known coach, and at one point asked if he had a purpose statement for his life. He quickly responded, "I've always wanted to know what my real purpose is." We asked questions and took notes for about half an hour, and then helped him discover and document his purpose. We boiled this down to a single memorable statement. I saw him several weeks later and the first thing he spoke to me was his purpose statement. His face was radiant!

LET'S PRAY:

Jesus, we need your help! Without you, we worship our work. As we look for the one, our only hope is to walk in the shadow of your wings. Help us listen for your slightest whisper and open our eyes to your purpose for the one you have brought into our lives. Please help us know when it is time to plant seeds and when it is harvest time.

DISCUSS:

Do you have a purpose statement for your life?

Have you ever helped someone receive a revelation of their purpose?

What is the role of repentance in fulfilling your purpose?

"Repent, then, and turn to God, so that your sins may be wiped out, that times of refreshing may come from the Lord" (Acts 3:19).

How do you know when you are speaking to a Manfred and when you are speaking to a Uriah?

How does Paul demonstrate the power of purpose?"

"But my life is worth nothing to me unless I use it for finishing the work assigned me by the Lord Jesus—the work of telling others the Good News about the wonderful grace of God" (Acts 20:24).

As I look for the one who needs purpose, how do I become more like Jesus?

Looking For The One
WHO NEEDS TO ABIDE

"The heart of Jesus cries out, 'Come to me to stay with me.'"
Andrew Murray

ONE DAY AT LITTLE LEAGUE a new kid walked onto the field. He was overweight and looked unsure of himself. Within moments the gang sensed his weakness. Soon a group of boys gathered around and decided that his new nickname was soggy maggots. He stood head bowed, defenseless. As we waited for the guys to leave, his hands picked at his glove. When he finally looked up, tears were running down his dusty face.

"What's your name?" I asked.

There was a long pause, and he said, "Danny."

I told Danny that I would never call him by the other name, and then we talked about baseball. Danny was a loner at school, but I went out of my way to speak to Danny. I noticed that his face would brighten every time I called his name.

Several years later, at college, my mom sent me a newspaper clipping with Danny's obituary. As I looked at Danny's picture, I wondered about his brief life. I remembered the lies spoken to Danny and felt a wave of conviction.

I had encouraged Danny, but I had never spoken to him about Jesus.

All these years later, I was driving toward Target Field on a beautiful Sunday morning. On the seat beside me was a brown paper bag. Inside the bag was a branch that was green with life. Next to it was a branch that was dry and brittle. This branch died long ago.

As I approached the stadium, I second-guessed the brown paper bag. These were professional athletes and major league umpires. The branches were the kind of thing that you bring to a Sunday School class. As I thought and prayed, it occurred to me that the branches are the kind of thing that Jesus would have pointed to as he shared these words:

> *"As the branch cannot bear fruit by itself, unless it abides in the vine, neither can you, unless you abide in me. I am the vine; you are the branches. Whoever abides in me and I in him, he it is that bears much fruit, for apart from me you can do nothing"* (John 15:4-5, ESV).

On the one hand, Jesus is telling simple stories and including object lessons that even children can understand. On the other hand, his teaching changed the world.

I decided to bring along the branches.

My Sunday mornings include separate chapels for the home and visiting teams and a chapel for the umpires. We talk at each chapel about what it means to have a life that matters. We discuss living for something more than baseball and leaving a lasting legacy. But according to Jesus, none of this is possible on our own. Apart from Jesus, we can do nothing of eternal value. Jesus is the source of life. He is the vine, and we are the branches.

Connected to the vine, we are alive and fruitful.

Disconnected from the vine, we are dead and unfruitful.

As I laid the branches on the table, we talked about the characteristics of a dead branch:

- I've heard about Jesus, but I've never committed to him.

- I think of Jesus at Christmas and Easter but am unaware of him the rest of the year.

- My lifestyle is not pleasing to him, and I am not willing to adjust my life to honor him.

- Instead of bearing fruit for the Kingdom of God, my life is all about me.

Next, we talked about branches that are alive:

- I have repented of my sin and turned to Jesus for his forgiveness and new life.

- I think of Jesus daily. Sometimes it is only a whisper, but I listen to his voice.

- I'm far from perfect, but when Jesus convicts me, I yield to his authority.

- My life is fruitful because it is my joy to serve the people around me.

As we looked down at the two branches, it was time for the question of the day: *Which branch are you?*

If you are a dead branch, there is a word of life for you. "If we declare that Jesus is the Son of God, we live in union with God, and God lives in union with us" (1 John 4:25, GNT).

Several weeks later, I walked through the stadium's lower level, and I heard a voice behind me. When I turned around, I recognized one of the umpires who had been in chapel that Sunday. There was no time for a conversation, but there was time for a statement.

"That dead branch changed my life."

There are people all around you who are desperate for the life of Jesus. From the little leagues to the major leagues, they know what life looks like as a dead branch. They know something is broken, but they don't know how to fix it.

The focus of this book is looking for the one.

But the heart of this book is Jesus.

Because looking for the one is impossible without abiding in the One. This is Jesus looking for the one through you.

REFLECT:

Am I abiding in Christ?

Do I tend to compartmentalize my faith, or am I aware of Jesus throughout my day?

Am I a branch connected to Christ?

EQUIP:

How do I look for the one who needs to abide?

DISCERNMENT: Instead of behavior, focus on discernment. Discerning if someone is dead or alive spiritually protects you from judging the dead branches around you.

BE ORDINARY!: You may not be a pastor or a missionary, but you are qualified if you are walking with Jesus. Peter and John boldly testified of Jesus because they had been with Jesus. "They could see that they were ordinary men with no special training in the Scriptures. They also recognized them as men who had been with Jesus" (Acts 4:13).

INVITE PEOPLE TO FOLLOW JESUS: "And now, just as you accepted Christ Jesus as your Lord, you must continue to follow him" (Colossians 2:6).

WALK WITH JESUS as he whispers, "Come to me, all of you who are weary and carry heavy burdens, and I will give you rest" (Matthew 11:28).

LET'S PRAY:

Jesus, please keep me close to your side because my greatest joy is to walk with you. I ask for discernment so that I can speak your life into the dead branches all around me. May I become your hands and feet.

DISCUSS:

What does it mean to abide?

"I am the vine; you are the branches. Whoever abides in me and I in him, he it is that bears much fruit, for apart from me you can do nothing. If anyone does not abide in me he is thrown away like a branch and withers; and the

branches are gathered, thrown into the fire, and burned" (John 15:5-6).

What are some of the advantages of abiding?

"He who dwells in the shelter of the Most High will abide in the shadow of the Almighty" (Psalm 91:1, ESV).

How does abiding affect our prayer life?

"If you abide in me, and my words abide in you, ask whatever you wish, and it will be done for you" (John 15:7).

Does resting or sabbath make you feel guilty?

Is there anything in your schedule that hinders your ability to abide in Christ?

Is there someone in your life like Danny who needs a defender?

As I look for the one who needs to abide, how am I becoming more like Jesus?

Looking For The One
WHO SERVES YOU
AT 30,000 FEET

"Jesus, Savior, pilot me, Over life's tempestuous sea; Unknown waves before me roll, Hiding rock and treach'rous shoal; Chart and compass came from Thee; Jesus, Savior, pilot me."

Edward Hopper, 1871

AS YOU LOOK FOR THE ONE on your flight, don't forget the men and women serving you! Even before Covid-19, serving as a pilot or flight attendant could be very stressful.

Several years ago, the man next to me introduced himself as a pilot specializing in non-stop flights to Asia. As we got to know each other, I asked him if there were any close calls, and he shared the numerous times that the crew had to react to weather or mechanical issues. Then I asked, "What is your most memorable flight? What is the funniest or craziest thing that has ever happened?" He told me about the day an older woman hired him to fly a twin-engine plane over the mountains. She told him it didn't matter when he asked about a destination. She would empty her husband's ashes some-where over his favorite mountain range.

"She sat next to me, holding this urn, and we flew along in awk-ward silence. Finally, I directed her to open a small window when the mountains appeared below. As she removed the urn's top, his ashes were sucked out and deposited all over the plane.

"She turned to me, 'Henry was always a handful,' and laughed uncontrollably. When we got back to the hangar, I dusted myself off and told the guys to go and find a shop vac!"

Now it was time to ask a question that might open up the door to a heart. "What is the greatest challenge in your career?" There was a long pause. My new friend quietly said, "Alcohol."

For the next 15 minutes, he described the loneliness of being a single man in strange cities and turning to alcohol to cope with the stress. He added, "So far, I've never had a drink the day before a flight." A principle came to mind from Psalm 62, and we read these verses together:

> *"For God alone my soul waits in silence; from him comes my salvation. He alone is my rock and my salvation, my fortress; I shall not be greatly shaken"* (Psalm 62:1-2, ESV).

I walked him through the gospel and gave him my contact information. I shared that no person or substance can take the place of Jesus and that God alone is the source of our joy and peace. As I write these words, I have yet to hear from him.

When he comes to mind, I pray for his loneliness, and I pray for his salvation. I have hope because he dared to tell the truth and was open to hearing the truth. We know that God's Word never returns empty!

> *"It is the same with my word.*
> *I send it out, and it always produces fruit.*
> *It will accomplish all I want it to,*
> *and it will prosper everywhere I send it"*
> (Isaiah 55:11).

God can cause a pilot to sit next to you, or he can cause a pilot to walk with you. One summer afternoon, as I walked around a lake in a large city, I asked Jesus to show me the one. Moments later, a man stepped out of his home and began to walk next to me. We were stride for stride, and within a few steps, he told me of his love for Jesus. He shared about life as an international pilot and all of the Bibles he carried to believers in Asia. We prayed together for his "mission trips" and his passion for seeing revival come to his city. As we were about to say goodbye, he described what it was like to walk into an underground church with a Bible and hand a believer their first copy of God's Word. The choice is so clear:

> Without Jesus, we are looking for hope at the bottom of a bottle.

> With Jesus, we carry a message of hope.

My friend Larry travels internationally for his business and has regular opportunities to share his faith in Christ. But something happened last year that made him more intentional.

After a long flight, Larry came home and noticed that his lower leg was in pain. As a red-blooded male, Larry decided that the best course of action was to go for a run. The run went well, but the blood clot from his leg reached his lungs when he walked in the door. The only thing that saved Larry was that his son "happened" to be downstairs, and when he heard him crash to the floor, he immediately called 911.

The doctors took it a step further. They explained to Larry that he struck the floor at precisely the right angle when he fell. The impact dislodged the double thrombosis just enough to keep him alive until the paramedics arrived. As Larry shared about his brush with death, he spoke with clarity. "Jesus spared my life so I can spend my life sharing the gospel."

It has been my habit to stretch my legs during a long flight, but after hearing Larry's story, I am a man on a mission for periodic trips to the back of the plane. Flight attendants have work to be done, but if you wait for the right moment, you can arrive at the back of the plane when they are not under as much pressure.

On a flight to Florida, I arrived in the back as a veteran flight attendant was sharing her war stories with two young ladies who had been working for a few months. As we got to know one another, I shared about PraiseLive and some of the life-change stories from our listening family. The older flight attendant showed no interest, but one of the newcomers shared that she had just moved to the Twin Cities and was looking for a church home. A follower of Jesus!

I shared with her the prayer that has changed my life. "Jesus, show me the one." Then I asked, "What do you think would happen if you were to approach every flight looking for just one person to bless?" We bowed our heads at 30,000 feet and prayed for a supernatural ability to look for the one. Several weeks later, I received this email:

Hi, Pastor McIver!

I hope this message finds you well! I had the pleasure of being your flight attendant a few weeks back on my flight from Fort Myers to Minneapolis. It was so wonderful meeting you and your lovely family. I just wanted to share with you since our encounter; I've kept the challenge of seeking my "one" on each flight. It truly has become a treasure hunt for me, and I must say, it's given me a different kind of excitement to sign into work each morning. Pastor, I just wanted you to know that I was truly blessed when you prayed over me in the back galley. I truly felt the Lord's presence that day, and it could not have come at a better time in my life. God is not finished with me yet, and meeting you was confirmation that I am where I am supposed to be. I'm going to continue doing the Lord's work!

Sometimes the one we meet at 30,000 feet has an unforgettable testimony. I was on a flight to Florida and met a flight attendant named Sarah. Her incredible smile was filled with joy, so I asked a couple of questions about her spiritual journey. Sarah grew up in Japan with no connection to the Church or Jesus, but she had a hunger for God.

One day Sarah was having lunch at McDonald's and was suddenly overcome with desperation to know God. She prayed, "God, if you are real, show yourself to me." Seconds later, a pastor walked in and asked if she would like to know Jesus. She went into the restroom and got down on her knees to give her heart to Christ. Sarah shared what happened next. "As I was on my knees praying, the intercom system started playing this beautiful song about Jesus and his love for me. The song went on and on until suddenly I realized the song was referring to me by name. Jesus was singing over me!"

Someone around you is praying, "God, if you are real, show yourself to me."

Someone is waiting for you to walk into their life and Jesus is longing to sing over them.

REFLECT:

Imagine for a moment the look on the face of Jesus as he is watching someone like Sarah.

Now imagine the look on his face when he sees your willing heart to speak to her.

EQUIP:

How do I look for the one at 30,000 feet?

WATCH AND PRAY: When you have a moment with Jesus, ask him to show you his heart for those who serve us. Ask the one who washed his disciple's feet, "Why are servants a reflection of Jesus?"

TAKE A WALK: On your next flight, ask the Lord which crew member is on his heart. Ask him to show you when to get up and stretch your legs. Pray for the right questions and the right words to bring a revelation of Jesus at 30,000 feet. On your next walk, ask Jesus to order your steps so that you are in step with his will.

LET'S PRAY:

Jesus, forgive me for the times I have murmured against those you have placed in my life to bless and serve me. Forgive me for impatience and times I have been ungrateful. Please show me the one who is desperate for you. I desire to go on treasure hunts with you!

DISCUSS:

How does sharing the gospel nourish us?

"Then Jesus explained: 'My nourishment comes from doing the will of God, who sent me, and from finishing his work. You know the saying, "Four months between planting and harvest." But I say, wake up and look around. The fields are already ripe for harvest'" (John 4:34-35).

How is someone convicted of sin? Who is the Helper?

> *"Nevertheless, I tell you the truth: it is to your advantage that I go away, for if I do not go away, the Helper will not come to you. But if I go, I will send him to you. And when he comes, he will convict the world concerning sin and righteousness and judgment"* (John 16:7-8, ESV).

How do we become a child of God?

> *"But to all who believed him and accepted him, he gave the right to become children of God"* (John 1:12).

How do you feel about talking to strangers?

How do we interact with people in ways that they trust us with their secrets?

How do we see people as treasures?

As I go on treasure hunts, how do I become more like Jesus?

Looking For The One
WHO NEEDS TO TRUST

"For I know the one in whom I trust, and I am sure that he is able to guard what I have entrusted to him until the day of his return."

2 Timothy 1:12

THE ALTAR IS PACKED with college students as I finish my Chapel message. Many of them are on their knees. One young man catches my eye as we pray over those who have come forward. He is the last to approach the altar, but as he begins to kneel, he abruptly backs away. He shakes his head as he walks to the back of the sanctuary.

But instead of walking out the back door, he turns around again and walks slowly back to the altar. His whole body is shaking as he begins to kneel. But once again, he backs away. This time his face appears to be angry.

As we watch and pray, suddenly, he throws himself facedown on the altar and begins to weep. Half an hour later, we find out why. About a year ago, he was in a vehicle with his fiancèe during a head-on collision. His life was spared, but his fiancèe died in his arms.

Today is the first time since the accident that he has been to an altar. More importantly, this is the day his trust in Jesus is restored.

At this chapel service, I shared a story that made no sense to me for many years. It seemed like God was being unfair to Moses. First, the background:

Moses never volunteered to be God's spokesperson or lead the people to the promised land. He told God, "O Lord, I'm not very good with words... I get tongue-tied, and my words get tangled" (Exodus 4:10). God responded by telling him, "I will be with you as you speak, and I will instruct you in what to say" (Exodus 4:12).

Moses agrees to God's plan, confronts Pharaoh, parts the Red Sea, and retires to play golf at Pebble Beach. (Not exactly.) After the Red Sea, he led the people out into the Desert of Zin. "There was no water for the people to drink at that place, so they rebelled against Moses and Aaron" (Numbers 20:2).

"The Lord said to Moses, 'You and Aaron must take the staff and assemble the entire community. As the people watch, speak to the rock over there, and it will pour out its water. You will provide enough water from the rock to satisfy the whole community and their livestock.'

"So Moses did as he was told. He took the staff from the place where it was kept before the Lord. Then he and Aaron summoned the people to come and gather at the rock. 'Listen, you rebels!' he shouted. 'Must we bring you water from this rock?' Then Moses raised his hand and struck the rock twice with the staff, and water gushed out. So the entire community and their livestock drank their fill.

"But the Lord said to Moses and Aaron, '*Because you did not trust me* enough to demonstrate my holiness to the people of Israel, you will not lead them into the land I am giving them!'" (Number 20:7-12, emphasis mine)

When we understand how God views trust, we understand this story. The community did not trust God, so they died in the wilderness. Instead of speaking to the rock, Moses struck the rock. The price of his distrust was the promised land.

As I've mentioned previously, my childhood bedroom was adjacent to our family's kitchen. Mom and Dad would talk about the unpaid bills and the financial pressure at night. As I listened, I became worried. Then I became afraid. Then I lost my trust. I was sure that God was not going to take care of me. I could never have a marriage and family because I would never be able to provide for a family.

When I joined the team at PraiseLive in 1985, my salary was $12,000 a year. As Sherrie and I began our family, we started to have late-night conversations in our kitchen about finances. We were working two jobs; then we had three jobs. At times we had four jobs and were getting further and further behind. I was fighting exhaustion and fighting my fear that God is not able.

In 1998, I had the experience of reading *With Christ in the School of Prayer* by Andrew Murray. I was stunned. I pulled out my prayer journal, and all I saw were pages filled with requests for provision. I was praying for months for funds to purchase tires for the car. But the life of prayer that Andrew described was a life of praying for his Kingdom. Praying for "daily bread" was part of prayer, but the secret to prayer was asking God what was on his heart.

I began to pray intently about the Kingdom of God. One night I was awakened and frightened by the presence of God. My room felt like it was illuminated. I managed to make my way to my office and spent the next several hours on my face. What was on God's heart was a global media platform for his presence. He invited me to change our format to worship, the Word, and prayer. He spoke to me about broadcasting across Africa. Then he invited me to ask him to confirm his word to me. "Ask me for a gift of $500,000, but tell no one."

When you have an area where you don't trust God, this is the area where he reveals himself as trustworthy. My secret fear is lack of provision, and God knows that I cannot accomplish his purpose for my life if I do not trust him.

As I knelt to pray, there was a calm assurance that I was praying for something on God's heart. It didn't matter that we were a rural ministry with headquarters surrounded by a cornfield. I said "Yes" to the invitation and asked for the confirmation.

Several weeks later, I received a phone call from someone who used to live in Minnesota and now lives over a thousand miles away. He was coming through the Twin Cities and asked if we could have dinner. He looked at me and said, "I was sitting on my deck, and the Lord told me that you had accepted an invitation from him. He told me that I was to confirm the invitation." With that, he slid a check across the table.

That night Sherrie and I got down on our knees. There was no celebration as we looked at a check for $400,000. But there was prayer because of the weight of the responsibility God was calling us to. The only puzzling part was the difference in the amount of the gift. The Holy Spirit had been so specific about the vision and the confirmation. The next day I received a call. "I missed God on the amount. I'm sending you another check."

When the FedEx envelope arrived, I opened it fully expecting a check for $100,000. This check was for $300,000. Then the still small voice of the Holy Spirit. "What I am asking you to build is dear to my heart."

I didn't know that we would wait twenty years for this vision to unfold. But in the waiting, I would remember the encounter with Jesus and the gifts that confirmed the vision. Today PraiseLive is available across almost all of Africa and the Middle East via satellite. We invite people to experience Jesus on FM signals across Africa.

Jesus is always worth the wait.

This is what I know about your life. If you ask Jesus what is on his heart, he will reveal something dear to his heart. He will also reveal something hidden in your heart. As you wait for the vision, Jesus is waiting for you.

Whenever I share about Moses and the promised land, I bring along a large iron wedge that I have used when cutting wood. I explain that Satan's goal is to drive a wedge between our heart and God's heart. But for the wedge to have any power, the wedge needs an entry point.

The entry point is the first time you believe that your Father is not trustworthy. Satan knows that if you believe God is not trust-worthy, you will not believe what he says to you. This lie is the entry point for a thief whose goal is your destruction. "The thief comes only to steal and kill and destroy..." (John 10:10).

We might think that our life is about accomplishing some-thing for God. But God's priority is always our heart. "Today when you hear his voice, *don't harden your hearts* as Israel did when they rebelled, when they tested me in the wilderness. There your ances-tors tested and tried my patience, even though they saw my miracles for forty years. So I was angry with them, and I said, *'Their hearts always turn away from me.* They refuse to do what I tell them.' So in my anger I took an oath, 'They will never enter my place of rest'" (Hebrews 3:7-11, italics mine).

It costs something to trust God. You stand in the desert, so thirsty that you want to go back to Egypt. But it costs far more not to trust him.

Your destiny is a land of promise you receive from your Father if you dare to trust him.

REFLECT:

When was the first time I believed my Heavenly Father was not trustworthy?

EQUIP:

How do I look for the one who needs to trust?

FOCUS ON THE FIRST PLACE: I spoke on this topic on a Sunday morning and invited people to come forward for healing. As we began to pray, the lines grew longer and longer. People waited 90 minutes to pray about the first time they believed their Father was not trustworthy. We prayed about divorce, abuse, eating disorders, and cancer. One young lady shared that she had come to church intent on taking her life when she returned home. Instead of taking her life, she gave her life at the altar.

LOOK TO HIM: We gently guide the gaze of one who cannot trust until they see the face of Jesus. "Want of trust is at the root of almost all our sins and all our weaknesses; and how shall we escape it but by looking to Him and observing His faithfulness? How many estimate difficulties in the light of their own resources, and thus attempt little and often fail in the little they attempt! All God's giants have been weak men, who did great things for God because they reckoned on His being with them" (Hudson Taylor).

FOLLOW THE TRAIL: A trail of poor decisions begins with the first decision to not trust God. As you follow the trail, you are searching for a broken heart that Jesus longs to heal. "Trust in the Lord with all your heart; do not depend on your own understanding. Seek his will in all you do, and he will show you which path to take" (Proverbs 3:5-6).

BUILD TOGETHER: Once Jesus begins to heal a heart, it's time to begin building on the foundation of Christ. "As the Scriptures say, "I am placing a cornerstone in Jerusalem, chosen for great honor, and anyone who trusts in him will never be disgraced" (1 Peter 2:6).

LET'S PRAY:

Jesus, I ask that you would open my eyes to the first place I lost sight of you. I pray that you would heal my heart and gently guide me to my land of promise. Even as you have declared, "Let there be light," please declare, "Let there be life!"

DISCUSS:

Moses was forbidden from entering the promised land, so why was he invited to stand with Jesus in the promised land?

"About eight days later Jesus took Peter, John, and James up on a mountain to pray. And as he was praying, the appearance of his face was transformed, and his clothes became dazzling white. Suddenly, two men, Moses and

Elijah, appeared and began talking with Jesus" (Luke 9:28-30).

When it comes to trust, what is at stake?

"This is what the Lord says: 'Cursed are those who put their trust in mere humans, who rely on human strength and turn their hearts away from the Lord. ... But blessed are those who trust in the Lord and have made the Lord their hope and confidence. They are like trees planted along a riverbank, with roots that reach deep into the water. Such trees are not bothered by the heat or worried by long months of drought. Their leaves stay green, and they never stop producing fruit'" (Jeremiah 17:5-8).

How do we talk to Jesus about our distrust?

"O my people, trust in him at all times. Pour out your heart to him, for God is our refuge" (Psalm 62:8).

What is dear to God's heart?

"For I have chosen this Temple and set it apart to be holy—a place where my name will be honored forever. I will always watch over it, for it is dear to my heart" (2 Chronicles 7:16).

As I look for the one who needs to trust, how do I become more like Jesus?

Looking For The One
WHO NEEDS TO
RECEIVE THE GIFT

*"Without Christ, you can do nothing, and you are nothing,
and you have nothing. Come to Jesus as you are, and
put your trust in him, and then all things are yours."*

Charles H. Spurgeon

IT HAD BEEN A WONDERFUL morning of meetings and prayer, but now a massive traffic jam. There was a chance we would miss our flight to Minneapolis. But as we neared the Denver airport, I remembered a spiritual principle. In the Kingdom of God, delays are divine opportunities. I breathed a prayer, "Jesus, show us the one at this airport who needs you."

The good news is that we made it to our gate on time. The bad news? Our flight was delayed and then delayed again. As United served us complimentary snacks, I joined a large contingent of people watching the Bears and Packers on Monday Night Football.

As I watched the game, I felt impressed to move to a different part of the gate. Now a loudspeaker crackled to life. "The good news is that the mechanical issue is fixed. The bad news is that now we have a flat tire."

The voice next to me was barely a whisper. "I'll never make my appointment." I turned and saw the look of concern on a woman's face. She saw the question on my face. "I have a medical appointment for my husband in downtown Minneapolis. It's for his brain tumor." After a few words of introduction, Rose showed me the MRI of Michael's tumor and then shared about her faith in Christ. Rose shared her concern for Michael's spiritual life when I asked about Michael's faith.

One of my favorite ways to share the gospel is The Salvation Poem.

> *Jesus, you died upon a cross*
> *And rose again to save the lost*
> *Forgive me now of all my sin*
> *Come be my Savior, Lord, and Friend*
> *Change my life and make it new*
> *And help me, Lord, to live for you*

I gave Rose a copy of the poem, and as we began to board the plane, we prayed for Michael's appointment and salvation. A guy wearing a Packers jersey joined our circle and bowed his head as we prayed.

Rose contacted me the following day to let me know that Michael and their daughters were awake and waiting for her when she arrived home in the middle of the night. She shared with Michael about our conversation and gave him the poem. I kept in touch with Rose and found out that the family was coming to a Twins game on a Sunday afternoon. Michael's brain surgery was taking place on the following day.

When the Twins are home on a Sunday morning, I host three chapel services. One for the Twins, one for their opponent, and one for the umpires. At all three services, I shared Michael's story and the spiritual battle for his life. "Guys, Michael is sitting somewhere in the outfield, and in a few minutes, I'm going to go meet with him and invite him to surrender his life to Christ. Today may be my only chance to speak to him in light of his surgery." The men bowed their heads in all three chapel services and prayed for Michael's salvation.

After chapel, Rose texted me their location, and I met Michael's beautiful daughters, Molly, Sammi, and Hannah.

When looking for the one, there are times when you take years to develop a friendship and slowly share your faith in Christ. But when it's the day before brain surgery, it is time for the direct approach.

"Michael, I need to know if you have a relationship with Jesus?" Michael glanced down and said he would prefer to talk about God after the surgery. He added, "I just hope that the good outweighs the bad in the end." When I tried to share that salvation is a gift we receive, the conversation came to a standstill. The game was about to start, and we were just about out of time.

As I prayed, I felt someone looking at me. Out of all the places at Target Field where Rose could have purchased tickets, she "happened" to buy seats in the row adjacent to the bullpen. Incredibly, their seats were on the end of the row next to the bullpen.

The person looking at me was Bill "Skip" Evers, one of the Twins' bullpen coaches. Bill told me later that as he walked into the bullpen, "Something made me look up." Bill had just been praying for Michael at chapel, so he nodded his head when I pointed at Michael. He knew this was the guy! Skip got Michael's attention and tossed a ball in our direction. The toss came up short of the bleachers, and now several kids gathered around Michael, hoping for a baseball.

Bill didn't know that Michael has double vision. Bill didn't know that I was at a loss for words, but he was determined to throw a ball to Michael at this exact moment.

When you go looking for the one, you get a front-row seat to the pursuing love of Jesus. Standing behind Michael, I saw the kids swarming around him. Below me, I saw Bill standing 40' or 50' from Michael. Now I watched in wonder as the ball soared up and began to descend.

The throw was perfect.

Michael reached above his head with both hands and caught it. Michael cried out, "I caught it, I caught it!"

Then the Holy Spirit moved in.

"Michael, is that your ball?"

"Yes!"

"Why is that your ball?" Michael looked puzzled. "Did you buy it?"

"No."

"So why does it belong to you?"

"I caught it!"

"Michael, the delays for Rose's flight were not a coincidence. We met for a reason. Buying tickets next to the bullpen was not by chance. Moments ago, I was trying to explain that salvation is a gift we receive. The coach who just prayed for you in chapel looks up and notices you at that exact moment. He decides to throw you a ball. Jesus did all of this so that you would understand that salvation is not something you earn or purchase but a gift that you receive. It's not trying to measure up or be good enough. It's a gift.

"You just reach out and catch it by faith."

Michael's eyes exploded with light. "That's it?! I need to catch it?"

"Yes!"

Michael said what every baseball player has said when they look up.

"I got it! I got it!"

The moment Michael got it, he received it. He closed his eyes, bowed his head, and prayed, "Jesus, thank you for dying for me. Forgive my sins. I receive you as my Savior."

It didn't matter that a baseball game was about to start or that a crowd of people was watching us. Michael stood straight and tall and surrendered his life to Jesus. In front of his family, he committed his life to Christ. Amid the tears, we circled up and prayed together.

As they wheeled Michael into surgery the next day, he was holding two things.

In the one hand, a baseball.

In the other hand, The Salvation Poem.

Michael lived for over a year but then passed away. Rose invited me to say a few words at a reception in his honor. As Rose introduced me to her family and friends, person after person brought up what had happened at Target Field. They knew! Then I shared with the group how Michael had caught the ball and received the gift of salvation. I invited each person to be like Michael. Just reach out and receive the gift of Jesus. "Live a life filled with love, following the example of Christ. He loved us and *offered himself as a sacrifice for us,* a pleasing aroma to God" (Ephesians 5:2, italics mine).

Rose sent a beautiful note.

> *Dear David,*
>
> *What a blessing it has been to have "tripped over you" in the Denver airport! Thank you for helping Michael accept God in your special way. I know he was a bit of a challenge for you! You have been a true gift from God for me, knowing that Michael is now at peace and watching over us all.*
>
> *With gratitude.*
>
> *Rose*

As Michael reached up to catch a baseball, Jesus reached down to save him.

REFLECT:

Have I received the gift of salvation? Have I caught it?

Who do I know that needs to catch the gift of salvation?

EQUIP:

How do I look for one who needs to receive the gift?

SURRENDER MY SCHEDULE: When we surrender our plans to the Lord, it changes how we see delays and detours. "We can make our plans, but the Lord determines our steps" (Proverbs 16:9).

LIVE GENEROUSLY: As we live generously, it prepares someone's heart to receive the riches of Christ. "To me, though I am the very least of all the saints, this grace was given, to preach to the Gentiles the unsearchable riches of Christ" (Ephesians 3:8).

HUMBLY SHARE: As we humbly share how we received the gift, it opens the door for someone to receive salvation humbly. Our humility becomes an example of God's grace. "But God had mercy on me so that Christ Jesus could use me as a prime example of his great patience with even the worst sinners. Then others will realize that they, too, can believe in him and receive eternal life" (1 Timothy 1:16).

POWER OF TEAMWORK: Tap into the power of teamwork. Living in a community means that one of your friends is there to toss the ball at just the right time. "The Lord now chose seventy-two other disciples and sent them ahead in pairs to all the towns and places he planned to visit" (Luke 10:1).

LET'S PRAY:

Jesus, we rejoice in the gift of salvation. We declare that "God saved you by his grace when you believed. And you can't take credit for this; it is a gift from God" (Ephesians 2:8). Give us a fresh revelation of what it means to receive the greatest gift of all. As we yield our delays and even our mess-ups to you, allow us the honor of seeing eyes explode with light!

DISCUSS:

When it comes to the gospel, who is on your team?

"Finally, when we could stand it no longer, we decided to stay alone in Athens, and we sent Timothy to visit you. He is our brother and God's co-worker in proclaiming the Good News of Christ. We sent him to strengthen you, to encourage you in your faith, and to keep you from being shaken by the troubles you were going through" (1 Thessalonians 3:1-3).

How can "chains" spread the gospel?

> *"And I want you to know, my dear brothers and sisters, that everything that has happened to me here has helped to spread the Good News. For everyone here, including the whole palace guard, knows that I am in chains because of Christ. And because of my imprisonment, most of the believers here have gained confidence and boldly speak God's message without fear"* (Philippians 1:12-14).

How does unity spread the gospel?

> *"Every time I think of you, I give thanks to my God. Whenever I pray, I make my requests for all of you with joy, for you have been my partners in spreading the Good News about Christ from the time you first heard it until now. And I am certain that God, who began the good work within you, will continue his work until it is finally finished on the day when Christ Jesus returns"* (Philippians 1:3-6).

How does persecution spread the gospel?

> *"But the believers who were scattered preached the Good News about Jesus wherever they went"* (Acts 8:4).

Have you ever received a gift with strings attached?

What is "attached" to the gift of salvation?

Why do so many people believe that we have to earn salvation?

As I offer the gift of salvation, how do I become more like Jesus?

Looking For The One
WHO IS GOING TO HELL

> *"It is not a question of God sending us to hell. In each of us, there is something growing, which will be hell unless it is nipped in the bud."*
>
> **C.S. Lewis**

THE VAST STADIUM was suddenly quiet as the question hung in the air. "Are you willing to surrender your life to Jesus Christ?" Then the invitation to come forward. Over 50,000 men faced the choice between heaven and hell, and the convicting presence of God was everywhere.

I remember standing in the presence of God at this Promise Keepers gathering in Minneapolis. More specifically, I remember the battle taking place during the invitation. Several weeks before Promise Keepers, Sherrie encouraged me to invite a friend to the meeting. I thought about it—but was hesitant because I wondered if a Promise Keepers meeting would make him uncomfortable. I worried that asking him might cost me a deeply valued relationship.

I placed "invite your friend" on the back burner, and I forgot all about it as the days went by. But Sherrie did not forget—and several times gently reminded me to make the phone call. But each time I picked up the phone, I pictured myself wounding or offending him.

One of the things that I love about my quiet times with Jesus is that he tells me the truth when I ask him a question. On one occasion, I asked Jesus a question about my heart.

"Why am I so open about the gospel with strangers but hesitant when speaking to my friends?" Jesus whispered, "Because you worship approval instead of me. Approval is an idol in your life."

We think of idols as ancient relics, but an idol is anything we treasure instead of Jesus. The idol of approval feels good as our coworkers approve of our overwork. Idols whisper that approval is more important than truth. But the problem with idols is summarized by C.S. Lewis: "Idols always break the hearts of their worshipers."

The Apostle Paul understood that approval is a game we cannot win. "Obviously, I'm not trying to win the approval of people, but of God. If pleasing people were my goal, I would not be Christ's servant" (Galatians 1:10).

During the 1800s, George Müller cared for over 10,000 orphans, established over 100 schools, and offered education to 120,000 children. But before the Holy Spirit could speak to George about orphans, he had to speak to him about approval. In a journal entry, George Müller testifies:

> *"There was a day when I died,*
> *utterly died,*
> *died to George Müller and his opinions,*
> *preferences,*
> *tastes,*
> *and will,*
> *died to the world, its approval*
> *or blame of even my brethren,*
> *and friends*
> *and since then*

*I have studied only to
show myself approved unto God."*

George Müller died to the idol of approval, and at that moment, thousands of children were given life.

Now, as Promise Keepers was only a few days away, approval had to die so that my friend could live. As I repented for loving approval more than the lost, I picked up the phone. This time the call was effortless. As I began to explain about the conference, my friend interrupted me. "I'd love to go!"

Now we were standing side by side as the invitation for Christ was given. All around us, men were stepping into the aisle and making their way to the stadium floor. Now the prompting of the Holy Spirit.

"Tell him, 'If you want to go forward, I'll go with you.'"

Then, of course, the battle began to rage again. I imagined my comment offending him.

At this moment, something happened that had never happened before. As I closed my eyes, I saw my friend surrounded by flames, and his face was in anguish. He was in torment and screaming. It was a glimpse of hell.

I turned to my friend, "If you want to go forward, I'll go with you."

His response stays with me to this day: *"I was hoping you would say that. Let's go!"* We walked together, stood together, and prayed together as he gave his life to Christ. In case you are wondering, our friendship was never the same!

I know. Talking about fire and brimstone is a thing of the past. We are too sophisticated to bring up hell as we share the good news of Jesus. Yet the Bible is filled with references to a place of torment and separation from God. A place called hell.

Over and over, Jesus spoke about hell. In Luke 16:23, Jesus describes hell as a place of torment. In Matthew 25:30, he describes hell as outer darkness. To the people in New Testament times, Jesus compares hell to "Gehenna," a trash dump where worthless things are thrown away and then consumed in fire (Matthew 25:30).

The contrast between heaven and hell is sobering. Hell is a place of weeping, suffering, and gnashing of teeth. In heaven, there is no more suffering. Hell is a bottomless pit where you feel like you are falling forever. Heaven is safe and secure with walls that are two hundred feet thick! In hell, there is total darkness, while in heaven, there is no more night. In hell, you are hungry and never satisfied. Heaven features a river of life that brings healing. Hell is devoid of God's presence, while heaven is where you see God's face and are never separated from him.

I have heard testimonies where the primary reason cited for receiving Jesus was to escape the fires of hell. But the primary reason that we invite someone to follow Jesus is the pure delight of loving Jesus. The miracle of being adopted by him and receiving his Spirit to live within us!

As you look for the one, never hesitate to share the consequence of sin. As A.W. Tozer once said, "We need preachers who preach that hell's still hot, heaven's still real, sin's still wrong, and the Bible is God's Word." Most of all, never hesitate to share the gospel. "But how can they call on him to save them unless they believe in him? And how can they believe in him if they have never heard about him? And how can they hear about him unless someone tells them?" (Romans 10:14)

As followers of Jesus, let us declare that everyone deserves the opportunity to discover and worship Jesus. Let us consider this stirring challenge: "If sinners will be damned, at least let them leap to hell over our bodies. And if they will perish, let them perish with our arms about their knees, imploring them to stay. If hell must be filled, let no one go there unwarned or unprayed for." (Charles H. Spurgeon).

As I worry about a friendship, Jesus counts the cost.

As I treasure approval, Jesus treasures the lost.

REFLECT:

Who has God brought into my life that needs Jesus?

Do I want their approval more than their salvation?

Do I avoid sharing the truth of God's Word concerning hell?

EQUIP:

How do I look for the one going to hell?

THE PRESENCE OF GOD: Processing the issue of approval begins in the presence of God. In my case, the longing for approval stemmed from a belief that God disapproved of me. Before any rescue missions, spend time at the foot of the cross with the one who came to rescue you. "The resurrection means that God has accepted and approves of Christ's work on the cross. Therefore He accepts and approves of us!" (Nancy Leigh DeMoss)

CONSIDER ETERNITY: As a teenager, my Dad and I rode along in his pickup truck, and he asked me to imagine something. "Imagine that every 10,000 years, a sparrow flies up to Mount Everest and takes one peck at the mountain. When the mountain has been reduced to dust, eternity will have just begun." Then Dad said, "Eternity is too long to miss Jesus."

TEMPERATURE CHECK: If hell is really a consuming fire, then we need to take our spiritual temperature. "If there be any one point in which the Christian Church ought to keep its fervor at a white heat, it is concerning missions. If there be anything about which we cannot tolerate lukewarmness, it is the matter of sending the gospel to a dying world" (Charles H. Spurgeon).

KNEEL WITH JESUS: Amy Carmichael served Jesus in India for 55 years, and rescued thousands of children from sex slavery. She risked her life to save their lives because she knelt with Jesus. "Sometimes it was as if I saw the Lord Jesus Christ kneeling alone, as He knelt long ago under the olive trees. And the only thing that one who cared could do, was to go softly and kneel down beside Him, so that He would not be alone in His sorrow over the little children" (Amy Carmichael).

LET'S PRAY:

Jesus, you have commanded us to go and make disciples of all nations. I say "Yes" to this command! Forgive my apathy and the many times I have loved approval more than the lost. Change my heart, oh God. Open my eyes and break my heart for what breaks yours.

DISCUSS:

Why is approval so important to you?

Have you missed sharing the gospel because you were afraid of disapproval?

Does talking about hell make you uncomfortable?

Why do we have conversations about hell?

> *"Just as the weeds are sorted out and burned in the fire, so it will be at the end of the world. The Son of Man will send his angels, and they will remove from his Kingdom everything that causes sin and all who do evil. And the angels will throw them into the fiery furnace, where there will be weeping and gnashing of teeth. Then the righteous will shine like the sun in their Father's Kingdom. Anyone with ears to hear should listen and understand!"* (Matthew 13:40-43)

What is our responsibility to the lost?

> *"Rescue others by snatching them from the flames of judgment"* (Jude 23).

Who is God leading you to?

As I look for the one going to hell, how do I become more like Jesus?

Looking For The One
WHO NEEDS A
REVELATION OF JESUS

"The world operates on vision. God's people live by revelation."

Henry Blackaby

WHEN I ARRIVED at Bethel College as a freshman, it helped that my sister Janice had already paved the way. I knew several of her friends who had made weekend trips to our farm in western Minnesota. But walking up to my dorm room, I was still nervous. I was a farm boy with four wonderful sisters, but this was my first experience moving in with a band of brothers.

My roommate Steve was from the East Coast, and a few minutes after we shook hands, we headed down to the cafeteria. On the way, we passed a group of freshman girls, and my new roommate informed me in R-rated detail what he would like to do to each of them. I was stunned.

The next revelation was that Steve had decided that it was unnecessary to do any laundry or clean any pots and pans scattered around his bed. Our room became a tourist destination. Students from neighboring buildings stopped by to see the mold growing in his leftover rice and beans. Things finally reached a breaking point when several of us taped off his entire side of the room. We posted an ultimatum that none of his laundry or mold was allowed on my side of the room.

As the weeks went by, Steve became well known for something else. Whenever there was a late-night conversation, Steve was in the middle of it. His favorite topics were politics and theology. Steve was intelligent, persistent, and argumentative. He was particularly good at asking probing questions that left his challenger speechless. I was gradually aware that Steve did not know Jesus in a personal way.

I knew there was no way to win a debate with Steve, so I asked Jesus what to do. The answer came immediately. "Get on your knees, lay your hands on his bed, and ask me to visit him during the night." It took some courage, but I carefully cleared a small space in the dirty laundry. I knelt and placed my hands on the bed, inviting Jesus to reveal himself to Steve.

It was about 3:00 AM when a voice began to whisper my name. As I came to, I realized that the voice belonged to Steve. His voice shook as he said, "Dave, there is a presence in the room, and I don't know what to do." When I asked what he meant by a presence, Steve responded, "Someone is here."

Then I remembered my prayer. "Jesus, reveal yourself to Steve."

Do you remember the moment when Jesus revealed himself to you? You had heard about him or argued about him, but you had never met him. It is like the Old Testament character Job. After 37 chapters of discussions with his friends about God and suffering, Job has a revelation. "Then the Lord answered Job from the whirlwind: Who is this that questions my wisdom with such ignorant words? Brace yourself like a man, because I have some questions for you, and you must answer them" (Job 38:1-3).

The Lord asks a series of questions like the one in Job 38:12: "Have you ever commanded the morning to appear and caused the dawn to rise in the east?" Finally, the Lord said to Job, "You are God's critic, but do you have the answers?" (Job 40:2)

We can only try to imagine the look on Job's face as he goes from a critic to a humble worshipper. He finally cries, "I know that you can do anything, and no one can stop you... I had only heard about you before, but now I have seen you with my own eyes. I take back everything I said, and I sit in dust and ashes to show my repentance" (Job 42:1-6).

George Müller was known worldwide for his work in caring for orphans. In April 1874, when he was almost 69, George Mueller wrote about a revelation of Jesus: "'Delight thyself also in the Lord; and he shall give thee the desires of thine heart' (Psalm 37:4, KJV). I know what a lovely, gracious, bountiful Being God is, from the revelation which He has been pleased to make of Himself in His Holy Word; I believe this revelation; I also know from my own experience the truth of it; and therefore I was satisfied with God, I delighted myself in God; and so it came, that He gave me the desire of my heart." It was the revelation of Jesus that birthed the revelation of caring for thousands of orphans.

During the next hour, I listened in as Steve went from a critic to a worshipper of Jesus. Steve repented of his pride and arrogance. I shared God's Word and led him through a prayer of salvation as he dedicated his life to Jesus. As Steve invited Jesus into his life, our room was alive with the presence of the Almighty. We quietly sang together!

The next day Steve began to clean his side of the room. Then he walked around campus and repented to people that he had wounded or offended. Next, Steve started a Bible study for seekers to come and meet with Jesus. The question around campus was, "What happened to Steve?"

The answer was a revelation of Jesus.

REFLECT:

Have I received a revelation of Jesus?

Who needs a revelation of Jesus in their life?

EQUIP:

How do I look for the one who needs a revelation of Jesus?

BE A PART OF THEIR STORY: Jesus has a strategy to reach the one on your heart. He is at work opening their eyes, and as you walk into their life, Jesus is whispering, "Come and see." As you are part of their story, you become a part of their revelation. Now you hear their testimony, "The mystery was made known to me by revelation" (Ephesians 3:3, ESV). As you enter their story you are declaring God's story. As you declare God's Word there is a revelation of Jesus.

THE HOLY SPIRIT: As Jesus spoke to the disciples about his departure he shared: "And I will ask the Father, and he will give you another Advocate, who will never leave you. He is the Holy Spirit, who leads into all truth." (John 14:16-17) As you look for the one who needs a revelation, you are following the lead of the Holy Spirit!

SOMEONE IN YOUR LIFE IS A MESS: You are very aware of the dirt and "mold" in their life and how it impacts your family. No doubt, you've tried talking to them and even providing boundaries for interaction.

But have you asked Jesus what to do? Have you prayed for a revelation of Jesus? You may not physically kneel in their home and pray for them, but you can kneel in your home and pray.

SOMEONE IN YOUR LIFE IS A PERFECTIONIST: You walk into their home and are afraid to touch anything. You walk into their life and are afraid to get close to them. As you pray for their revelation of Jesus, be prepared for something perfect to begin to unravel. Be prepared to see a spirit of performance replaced with a spirit of adoption.

LET'S PRAY:

Jesus, I need you! I've debated, advised, and provided boundaries, but none of that is a substitute for a revelation of you. Forgive me for focusing on their mess or perfectionism and losing sight of their heart. The God of this world blinds the minds of those who don't believe, but you can open the eyes of their heart! Jesus, be revealed!

DISCUSS:

What is the role of the Holy Spirit in revealing Jesus?

"The Holy Spirit will not let you be content in your blindness. He would not allow it for Paul, nor would He allow it for John Newton. Be assured He will not allow it for you. He longs to open the curtains and let in the light

that will make your world sparkle with all the bright colors of paradise" (David Jeremiah).

How is Jesus revealing his love for you?

"And may you have the power to understand, as all God's people should, how wide, how long, how high, and how deep his love is. May you experience the love of Christ, though it is too great to understand fully. Then you will be made complete with all the fullness of life and power that comes from God" (Ephesians 3:18-19).

Why does Jesus reveal himself to us?

"Who are you, lord? I asked. And the Lord replied, 'I am Jesus, the one you are persecuting. Now get to your feet! For I have appeared to you to appoint you as my servant and witness. Tell people that you have seen me, and tell them what I will show you in the future. And I will rescue you from both your own people and the Gentiles. Yes, I am sending you to the Gentiles to open their eyes, so they may turn from darkness to light and from the power of Satan to God. Then they will receive forgiveness for their sins and be given a place among God's people, who are set apart by faith in me" (Acts 26:15-18).

Do you feel prepared to respond to a question about salvation?

"The jailer called for lights and ran to the dungeon and fell down trembling before Paul and Silas. Then he brought

*them out and asked, 'Sirs, what must I do to be saved?'
They replied, 'Believe in the Lord Jesus and you will be
saved, along with everyone in your household.' And they
shared the word of the Lord with him and with all who
lived in his household"* (Acts 16:29-32).

Do you tend to be messy or a perfectionist?

Who needs a revelation of Jesus in your life?

As I look for the one who needs a revelation of Jesus,
how do I become more like Jesus?

Looking For The One
WHO SERVES YOUR FAMILY

> *"Lord, teach me to listen. The times are noisy and my
> ears are weary with the thousand raucous sounds which
> continuously assault them. Give me the spirit of the boy
> Samuel when he said to Thee, 'Speak, for Thy servant
> heareth.' Let me hear Thee speaking in my heart. Let me
> get used to the sound of Thy voice, that its tones may be
> familiar when the sounds of earth die away and the only
> sound will be the music of Thy speaking voice. Amen."*

A.W. Tozer

YEARS AGO, IF YOU ASKED what I thought of when you said "oil
change," I would say, "Free popcorn and watching classic programming like *The Price Is Right*." Oil changes were a chance to escape for
a moment and catch my breath. Those days are long gone.

Today I'm driving to the dealership for my oil change and
rehearsing staff members' names. I'm thinking about Trish and her
young daughter. I'm looking forward to hearing more about Mike's
dream of buying a home in the country. After Trish checks my car
in, I make my rounds with some treats I've brought along for the
team. Then I watch to see who is in God's appointment book.

There's always one.

I haven't prayed with anyone at the dealership or led anyone to Christ, but I met the new manager the other day, and as I began to introduce myself, he said, "I know who you are. You're the guy who is so nice to our staff." Then he asked about what was going on in my world as a pastor.

Sometimes the people who serve us come to our home. When we moved a few years ago, several rooms needed to be painted. When James arrived, he was all business. I stopped by a few times to give him water or a protein bar, but it was evident that James was focused on his work. I watched the surgical movements of his hands for a moment as he painted next to the ceiling. He was fast, and he was professional.

When Sherrie whispered to me, it was late afternoon. "I think we are supposed to serve James dinner." I've learned that when Sherrie says, "I think" regarding blessing someone, she might as well say, "Jesus told me."

James was hungry, and as he ate a warm meal, he began to tell us about his family. James began to open up when the conversation shifted to church and faith. I watched in wonder as Sherrie prayed for James and his family. Tears rolled down his face as Sherrie prayed over his life. We kept in touch, and he accepted our invitation to join us for a church service. James liked it so much that he invited his friends to church. All of his friends.

Sherrie said, "I think we are supposed to bring groceries to James' wife at Christmas time. He's out of town on an extended job." A few days later, Susan answered our knock at the door, and I saw her look from the groceries to Sherrie. She saw the love of Jesus.

A few weeks later, Sherrie sat next to Susan at church and presented her with her own Bible. She even gave her a highlighting pencil.

James is not just the guy you hired to paint a room. James and his family matter to Jesus.

As you look for the one who is serving your family, your most significant opportunities to share Jesus almost always come when you are busy and overwhelmed. Like when you are moving.

In our 38 years of marriage, Sherrie and I have moved a dozen times. The first eight or nine moves were friends and family affairs. Pickup trucks and flatbed trailers—scratch and dent specials. As we moved into our fifties, we started hiring some help. Five years ago, we moved, and Sherrie was looking at a website that lists cleaning companies in the Twin Cities. She was asking Jesus which one to hire. When she pointed to a company from St. Paul, I already know why they were coming to our home.

Because when you are looking for the one, Jesus tells you which one.

The next day a team of three young people arrived at our door and hit the ground running. I was delighted to find out that two of them had just come to St. Paul from Africa! I was exhausted and overwhelmed, but I knew it was time to go fishing as they finished up in the garage. I asked for a moment and began to share what a good job they had done. I complimented several specific things about their work and blessed each one. Then I asked if I could share for a moment about Jesus. "So many times we've heard about him, but we don't know him." All three nodded and smiled.

The Fisherman's Bible is a New Testament with five passages numbered and earmarked. The process is simple. You ask someone to read a verse and then ask what it means. You watch as people preach God's living Word to themselves. Someone will often read one of these verses and, without any prompting, reread it slowly. You can see the lights coming on!

One of the team read Ephesians 2:8: "For by grace, you are saved through faith, this is not from yourselves; it is God's gift—not from works, so that no one can boast." I asked one of the young men, "What does that mean?"

"It means that if the good outweighs the bad at the end of our lives, we make it into heaven." His co-worker jumped in, "Were you not listening to what you just read? Read it again!" This time he slowly read the words, "It is God's gift—not from works, so that no one can boast." He looked up in wonder and said, "It's a gift?" His friend declared, "Yes! It's not the good outweighing the bad. It's receiving the gift of salvation."

Now it was time to discover how to receive the gift of salvation. It was the young lady's turn to read, and she slowly declared, "If you openly declare that Jesus is Lord and believe in your heart that God raised him from the dead, you will be saved. For it is by believing in your heart that you are made right with God, and it is by openly declaring your faith that you are saved" (Romans 10:9-10).

Moments later, all three bowed their heads and prayed to invite Jesus to be their Savior and Lord. The remarkable thing was that they preached God's Word to themselves!

Like a little boy named Samuel, we listen for the voice of Jesus. As we listen, he gives us insight into the heart of the one serving us.

REFLECT:

How do I serve the one who serves my family?

EQUIP:

How do I look for the one who serves my family?

BE PREPARED: Resources like the Fisherman's Bible or the Salvation Poem are difference makers. At PraiseLive, we have given out over 100,000 copies of the Salvation Poem. At one point, I shared the gospel with the Fisherman's Bible, and nine out of ten people gave their lives to Jesus!

PRAY OVER PLUMBERS: When hiring someone to work for your family, ask Jesus who you should hire. Somehow, someway, He will show you the one. Ask the Lord to show you something about their hope and a future.

ADMIRE THEIR WORK: The one who paints our walls or repairs a roof has received a steady diet of criticism. It comes with the territory. But when you admire the work of their hands, it opens the door to their heart.

REMEMBER JESUS: "Have this mind among yourselves, which is yours in Christ Jesus, who, though he was in the form of God, did not count equality with God a thing to be grasped, but emptied himself, by taking the form of a servant, being born in the likeness of men" (Philippians 2:6-7).

LET'S PRAY:

Jesus, you came to seek and save us, but you also came to model servant leadership. Thank you for those who serve our families. I honor and bless them as a gift from you. Please open my eyes to their unique talents and open their hearts to the gift of salvation.

DISCUSS:

Have you ever hired someone, and the job did not go well? How did you respond?

Do you tend to point out what has gone wrong in life?

How does a guest in your home see what God has done?

> *"He has given me a new song to sing, a hymn of praise to our God. Many will see what he has done and be amazed. They will put their trust in the LORD"* (Psalm 40:3).

How do you prepare your heart for wonderful new relationships?

> *"So now we can rejoice in our wonderful new relationship with God because our Lord Jesus Christ has made us friends of God"* (Romans 5:11).

Who is Jesus asking you to walk beside?

> *"The Holy Spirit said to Philip, 'Go over and walk along beside the carriage'"* (Acts 8:29).

As I look for the one who serves my family, how do I become more like Jesus?

Looking For The One
HUNGRY FOR GOD'S WORD

"Heaven and earth will disappear, but
my words will never disappear."

Matthew 24:35

"HOW DO I BECOME the spiritual leader of my family?" As I look into Kurt's face, I see the fire in his eyes. This question matters deeply to him. Kurt Suzuki is a catcher for the Minnesota Twins and has yet to attend a chapel service. These words are the first that Kurt has ever spoken to me.

Kurt asks this question because his family has started reading God's Word. Kurt's family is reading God's Word because my wife loves God's Word.

When Sherrie is in the kitchen, she is listening to a sermon. As Sherrie walks down the hallway with her phone, I hear a message going by. But as much as Sherrie loves to listen to a message, her passion is to open and interact with God's Word. Sherrie loves ministries like Bible Study Fellowship.

When Sherrie leads a women's Bible Study, the goal is for the women to engage with the text. It's not time for a lecture. As Anne Graham Lotz has declared so many times: "It's time to open the book and ask, 'What does it say?' 'What does it mean?' 'What does it mean to me?'" Sherrie's Bible studies for the wives and girlfriends of the Twin players are held at the stadium and includes women raised in the Church and ladies who have never been to church. Years ago, Sherrie was about to begin her first Bible study when someone asked the first question. "Before we get started, could you clarify who God is? There are so many religions. Which God are we talking about?"

When the Twins signed Kurt, his wife Renee started coming to Bible studies. As Sherrie saw her hunger for God's Word, she gave her a Life Application Bible. As Sherrie got to know her daughter Malia, she felt prompted to provide her with a Children's Bible.

I happened to be there when Sherrie knelt in front of Malia and handed her a gift bag. Malia opened the gift, and now she was holding God's Word. Sherrie spoke to her about what was in her hands, and I saw the wonder in Malia's eyes. Then I saw the intensity. She was going to read this book!

Now Kurt was asking how to become the spiritual leader of his family. When I asked Kurt what had prompted the question, he broke into a huge smile.

"Because every day when I come home, Malia asks me to read her Bible to her."

I shared with Kurt that leading his family begins with giving his life to Jesus. "As you follow Jesus, you set the pace for your family. As you follow Jesus, you become a servant leader."

Kurt started attending chapels and Bible studies, and best of all gave his life to Jesus. One day Kurt shared his desire to be baptized. Kurt and Renee hosted a gathering at their home to publicly share their decision to follow Jesus. As I was about to baptize Kurt, someone came and stood at the edge of the pool. Someone wanted to be as close as possible to the action.

It was Malia.

Someone might look at a book and say, "It's only words." But our words matter. Winston Churchhill's last words were, "There is no hope." The last words of Jesus on the cross are a promise: "It is finished."

When followers of Jesus trust God's Word, there is authority and life change. There is the freedom to follow Jesus with abandon. "I am a Christian because God says so, and I did what he told me to do, and I stand on God's Word, and if the Book goes down, I'll go with it" (Billy Sunday).

As Renee is reading God's Word, Jesus is transforming her. As Renee is baptized, she testifies to new life in Christ. As Malia asks her dad to read God's Word, Kurt is preaching the gospel to himself.

In 2019 I watched the World Series between the Washington Nationals and the Houston Astros. I was hanging on every pitch, but I was not praying for a particular team to win. I know there are men who love Jesus on each team.

Kurt was at the plate facing Justin Verlander in game two of the world series. It was the 7th inning, and the score was 2-2. Kurt swung at a fastball, and the sound of bat meeting ball jolted me from my seat. Kurt's home run over the left-field wall gave the Nationals the lead. As Kurt was about to cross home plate, I saw him look up. Then I saw him point up. Then I thought of how Malia asked her dad to read God's Word. In the days that followed, Sherrie and I prayed for Kurt many times. We knew that there would be many opportunities to share the gospel.

You will probably not hit a home run in a World Series or share your faith with millions.

But you can give God's Word to a child.

REFLECT:

Whose life could be transformed by God's Word?

EQUIP:

How do I look for the one hungry for God's Word?

ONEHOPE: Years ago, Rob Hoskins of OneHope spoke at a church in the Twin Cities. As Rob shared the vision of giving the story of Jesus to every child on earth, I was mesmerized. As Rob shared stories of families and nations transformed by the Word of God, I was compelled to serve their ministry. In a meeting with Bob Hoskins and the leadership team of One-Hope, I offered a partnership between our ministries. Specifically, the Holy Spirit was offering them a global audience as a prayer covering.

Several people started to cry simultaneously, and then Bob explained why. Last week, Bob had told the staff that they had lost their prayer covering for the first time in their history. This is why *The Book of Hope* faced a wave of opposition or staff members faced a wave of personal attack. Bob had told the team that the ministry could not move forward until the Lord established a new prayer covering.

The Book of Hope is the story of Jesus, and it is customized for children around the world to understand the gospel and engage with God's Word. As you invest in OneHope, every dollar presents three children with *The Book of Hope*. Are the children being impacted? Yes!

But when children like Malia hold God's Word, they ask someone in their family to read it to them.

GIVE GOD'S WORD: Craig was a discouraged college student with no interest in Jesus, but a member of the Gideons gave him a New Testament. Craig opened God's Word and started reading. When he came to the book of Ephesians, he knelt and gave his life to Jesus. Now Craig Groeschel pastors Life Church in Oklahoma City. As this community plants churches, they now reach over 70,000 people each weekend. This church also launched the YouVersion Bible app, with over 500 million downloads. PraiseLive is honored to share content on this platform. Whenever I meet with the YouVersion team, I am reminded of what can happen when we go looking for the one who is hungry for God's Word!

STUDY THE SOIL: As you speak God's Word, you can discern if the Word is falling on rocky ground, among thorns, or on good soil (Luke 8:11-15).

TRUST AND OBEY: "Read God's Word because you love him. Do what it says because you trust him" (Dr. Tony Evans).

LET'S PRAY:

Jesus, as I open your Word, I ask that you would write it on my heart. I yield to the authority of your Word and release your Word to my family. I pray that you open my eyes to children who would love to receive your Word. I pray that you would anoint these children to carry God's Word to their families.

DISCUSS:

Why is God's Word a daily priority?

"For the word of God is alive and powerful. It is sharper than the sharpest two-edged sword, cutting between soul and spirit, between joint and marrow. It exposes our innermost thoughts and desires" (Hebrews 4:12).

Why do we declare God's Word over our life?

"For as the rain and the snow come down from heaven and do not return there but water the earth, making it bring forth and sprout, giving seed to the sower and bread to the eater, so shall my word be that goes out from my mouth; it shall not return to me empty, but it shall accomplish that which I purpose, and shall succeed in the thing for which I sent it" (Isaiah 55:10-11, ESV).

How do we pray God's Word over our life?

As you read the Word of God, some phrases and promises jump off the page. This is because God's Word is alive. As you speak these words, you release the seed of God's Word. You unleash the creative power of God. "...the heavens existed long ago, and the earth was formed out of water and through water by the word of God" (2 Peter 3:5, ESV).

Do you dare to believe that everything is possible?

> *"The wonderful thing about praying is that you leave a world of not being able to do something, and enter God's realm where everything is possible. He specializes in the impossible. Nothing is too great for His almighty power. Nothing is too small for His love"* (Corrie Ten Boom).

How is Jesus a declaration of God's Word to us?

> *"In the beginning the Word already existed. The Word was with God, and the Word was God. He existed in the beginning with God. God created everything through him, and nothing was created except through him. The Word gave life to everything that was created, and his life brought light to everyone. The light shines in the darkness, and the darkness can never extinguish it"* (John 1:1-5).

Why did Jesus make this statement to the devil: "We live by every word that comes from the mouth of God"? (Matthew 4:4)

As we look for the one hungry for God's Word, how do we become more like Jesus?

Looking for the One
WHO IS A STRANGER
AT YOUR DOOR

"Lord, when did we ever see you hungry and feed you? Or thirsty and give you something to drink? Or a stranger and show you hospitality? Or naked and give you clothing? When did we ever see you sick or in prison and visit you?" And the King will say, 'I tell you the truth, when you did it to one of the least of these my brothers and sisters, you were doing it to me!"

Matthew 25:37-40

AS A GUY with limited tech skills, I have had the honor of praying with countless people calling our home with customer support. I've even prayed with telemarketers. It never ceases to amaze me how strangers will open up about their stories and welcome a time of prayer.

One of my favorite phone calls was when Sherrie and I needed help with a laptop computer and ended up on the phone with customer support for about two hours. The young man who took our call was talented and intelligent. His manners were impeccable. At one point, when we were waiting for a software download, I asked about his family. It turns out that his mom and dad were pastors, but he had yet to embrace their faith. As he opened up about his questions, I pictured Mom and Dad praying for their son. As Sherrie prayed for him, I prayed silently that his mom and dad would one day look up and see their son walking with Jesus.

We can default to frustration over computers that don't work or join Jesus in looking for the one.

The Apostle Paul declared, "I am in chains now, still preaching this message as God's ambassador. So pray that I will keep on speaking boldly for him, as I should" (Ephesians 6:20). We live in a broken world, but as followers of Jesus, we are his ambassadors. We carry his presence into our schools, streets, and even our prisons. But as followers of Jesus, our homes are filled with the presence of God. When someone walks onto your property, they are encountering the presence of God. Barbara Rainey from Family Life Today has commented that our homes are an embassy for the King.

As I was writing this chapter, a van pulled up, and a young man was carrying a box to our front door. The Spirit of the Lord prompted me to meet him. How did I know? Because as I saw his face, I had compassion for him.

I met Ronald and thanked him for bringing us the package. As you know, most drivers are pressed for time and sometimes run back to their vehicles. But when you are looking for the one, Jesus makes time stand still. As Ronald turned to leave, I asked about his day, and he froze in place. Ronald shared about his busy day and that there were only two deliveries left. Ronald was no longer in a hurry because he sensed the presence of God.

As we walked toward the garage, Ronald began to share about his life. He had grown up in Nashville but moved to St. Paul because he needed "to get some things squared away." I asked about his family, and Ronald shared about his two daughters and son. His face beamed with pride as he shared about having a job and providing for his family.

"Have you found a church home yet?"

"No. I just haven't gotten around to it yet."

I gave him the names of two churches in the St. Paul area that came to mind and then gave Ronald a PraiseLive card. I shared about the worship music and the hope as you experience Jesus.

"Ronald, if you ever need prayer for your family, open our app and tap in your request. Within moments people from around the world can be praying for you."

"I need prayer."

"How can we pray for you?"

After a long pause, "I just need prayer."

When I pray for strangers, I picture them standing in front of Jesus. I try to imagine his heart for them. I try to see the look in his eyes as he looks into their eyes. Then I begin to pray. Over and over, I've heard people gasp or begin to break down as they sense the heart of Jesus for them. When you are standing in front of someone that Jesus is looking for, he prays through you.

We stood in our garage and prayed, and then Sherrie offered Ronald an ice-cold bottle of organic carrot juice. (Every family needs at least one health-conscious person.) Ronald waved her off. "Just had three red bulls." When I presented my favorite protein bar, Ronald held out his hand.

I told Ronald that we could see what a hard worker he was. Ronald nodded and turned away, but then he turned back. As we fist-bumped, he said, "No one has ever talked to me like this."

Sometimes looking for the one is listening to the knock at your door.

REFLECT:

Do I see the person knocking on my door as an interruption?

EQUIP:

How do I look for the stranger at my door?

SET APART YOUR HOME: You have people who are far from God around you, but they are not choosing to reject him. They don't know him. But, as these people walk onto your property, they can encounter the presence of God. These encounters are one of the reasons we live in homes set apart for the King of Kings.

A friend of mine received a call in the middle of the night. This family was hearing strange voices and then rustling sounds in the walls. When he came over, he placed a garbage can in the middle of the living room and announced it was time to take out the garbage. A few minutes later, this family had filled a garbage can with R-rated DVDs, magazines, and books. He received a phone call the next day that the oppression was gone and that they had slept like babies!

Your home is an embassy for the King. Ask Jesus if anything displeases him, and then anoint the corners of your home with oil, setting it apart for the presence of God. You can tape a verse next to your TV or computer screen: "I refuse to look at anything vile and vulgar" (Psalm 101:3). Now watch in wonder as people begin to encounter Jesus as they walk onto your property.

That call to customer support that you are dreading? Ask Jesus to connect your home and your heart to the one he is looking for.

FIGHT FOR MARGIN: Take a moment to reflect on the condition of your heart. Are you tense or overwhelmed? Do you have margin in your life? As you are honest about the state of your heart, now think back to the last time there was a knock at your door. The times we have been rude or even refused to open the door are symptoms of hearts that are overwhelmed. To move into margin is to become available to the stranger who needs Jesus.

IDENTIFY WITH STRANGERS: One of the reasons Jesus sends us a stranger is to remind us that without Jesus, we were strangers. Paul beautifully paints the contrast of life before and after Jesus in just one verse. "So then you are no longer strangers and aliens, but you are fellow citizens with the saints and members of the household of God" (Ephesians 2:19, ESV).

As we move into places of rest and remember what it's like to be a stranger, we live with open hearts and open doors. Now it is possible to "Cheerfully share your home with those who need a meal or a place to stay" (1 Peter 4:9).

LET'S PRAY:

Jesus, you know how I feel about interruptions and long conversations with customer service. You know the pressure I feel to get everything done. Today I choose to yield my schedule to you. *As I listen to a stranger, help me discern if they are strangers to you. Give me ears to hear.*

May this home be an embassy for our King of Kings. Now show me anything in this home that displeases you. Forgive me for anything I have looked at that was vile and vulgar. As people step onto our property, may they sense your presence and be drawn to you. Please give us the honor of welcoming friends and strangers around our table. Please help us to practice hospitality in a way that brings people into a relationship with you. As for me and my house, we will serve the Lord!

DISCUSS:

Have you gone on a trip where you felt like a stranger?

Do you see strangers as interruptions or opportunities?

Has a stranger ever been a guest in your home?

What are some of the blessings of helping strangers?

"Don't forget to show hospitality to strangers, for some who have done this have entertained angels without realizing it!" (Hebrews 13:2)

What would prompt a stranger to ask about your hope?

"And if someone asks about your hope as a believer, always be ready to explain it" (1 Peter 3:15).

How do I become more like Jesus as I look for the stranger at my door?

Looking For The One
WHO IS NEARING
THE FINISH LINE

"God works as He wills to overcome our rebellion. Like the wind that blows through the trees, He can neither be seen nor directed. He touches the heart. He breathes through snowflakes. The point is, He does it. He calls people to Himself, conceiving the new life in the Spirit in the secret place of the soul."

Chuck Colson

IT WAS A BUSY AFTERNOON, but I picked up the phone when a friend of mine called. He had just been alerted that a co-worker and several of his extended family were on their way to a Twins game that evening.

Most importantly, Pam would be at the game.

Pam is a passionate Twins fan who listens to almost every game and has been hoping to meet a member of the team someday. My friend shared that Pam had been born with cerebral palsy and that doctors had just given her six weeks to live because of a brain tumor.

But meeting a team member is not why he had called.

Pam did not have a relationship with Jesus.

In my years of serving with Baseball Chapel, I have never called and asked for tickets to a game or much less batting practice. But as I thought of Pam, I called the Twins Media Department. When Cori picked up the phone, I quickly explained the situation and asked if there was a way to purchase last-minute tickets. Cori quietly said, "No, but... we just had a group cancel for batting practice. How many tickets do you need?"

"Pam's family would need seven tickets."

"The group that canceled has seven tickets. There is no charge."

Cori and I met the family, and Cori shared with Pam that she would take her for a tour of the lower level so that she could see the door to the Twins' clubhouse. Then as Pam's wheelchair rolled past the visitors' locker room door, Cori took a right turn. Pam's eyes filled with wonder. She was on the field.

Cori guided her along the third baseline, and now she had a front-row seat to batting practice. As ball after ball flew into the bleachers, Pam's face was priceless.

When you are looking for the one, the Holy Spirit gives you insights so that the eyes of someone can be opened. As you wonder what to say, the Holy Spirit whispers secrets to you. "For his Spirit searches out everything and shows us God's deep secrets" (1 Corinthians 2:10).

When Jesus wants to reveal something to the one, he reveals a secret to us. The Holy Spirit was about to reveal something to Pam at this moment.

As the team was leaving the field, I made eye contact with Chris Gimenez. Chris is one of the Twins' catchers, and right on cue, he walked over to Pam and knelt in front of her. Chris spoke the first words of revelation. "Pam, I want you to know how beautiful you are."

Looking for the One

Now Twins pitcher Kyle Gibson was walking off the field, and as
he knelt in front of Pam, he spoke a word of life. "Pam, I want to
share something with you from Ephesians Chapter 2: 'For by grace
you have been saved through faith. And this is not your own doing;
it is the gift of God, not a result of works, so that no one may boast'"
(Ephesians 2:8-9). Then Kyle prayed a blessing over Pam.

Kyle and Chris did not know Pam's diagnosis or her spiritual
condition, but the Holy Spirit prompted them to speak to the secret
places of Pam's heart.

As the last player walked toward the dugout, the family turned
to leave. But Pam's quiet voice stopped us in our tracks. "Can I meet
Brian Dozier?"

As one of the guys headed to the locker room to find Brian, it was
my turn to kneel in front of Pam. "I am so happy that you can meet
some of the guys from your favorite team today. But I think the real
reason you came here is that Jesus wants to meet you. I want to share
a short poem with you that is a guide on how to meet Jesus and have
your own relationship with him. Would that be okay?"

I was looking into Pam's face, and I knew I had no idea what she
had endured. I couldn't imagine the courage it had taken to have
spent a lifetime facing cerebral palsy or what went through her mind
when she heard the word "tumor." It was almost imperceptible, but
as I looked into her beautiful eyes, she nodded.

The Salvation Poem has six lines of text, but we only made it to
the fourth line:

Jesus, you died upon a cross
And rose again to save the lost
Forgive me now of all my sin
Come be my Savior, Lord, and Friend
Change my life and make it new
And help me, Lord, to live for you

As I read, "Come be my Savior, Lord, and Friend," Pam's body began to vibrate. I sensed that Pam was experiencing a revelation of Jesus. "Pam, would you like Jesus to be all three of these in your life?

"*Savior* means every sin is forgiven. *Lord* means that you can trust him with your life. *Friend* means you'll never be forsaken."

There was no hesitation. Pam nodded her head and said, "Yes!"

I prayed with Pam and thanked Jesus for making her a new creation. As Pam said, "Yes," the vibration intensified. It was like watching an invisible current flow through her body.

When Pam opened her eyes, Twins second baseman Brian Dozier was kneeling in front of her.

All that Brian knew is that Pam had just made a decision for Christ. But as Brian spoke, he had secret information. "You've just made the best decision of your life. The best decision ever. Now go live. Go live!"

As Brian said, "Go live," another wave of the power of God touched Pam.

In the days that followed, I thought of Pam over and over. In all of my years of sharing The Salvation Poem, I had never seen someone physically react in that way. As Pam was inviting Jesus in, something had happened.

Something did happen. Three weeks later, my friend called again. Pam had gone in for a check-up which included another scan of the tumor.

The tumor was gone.

As I spend time with Jesus in heaven, I will ask him about Pam. My theory is that when Jesus came in, He told the tumor to get out. Pam did "Go live" for over a year, and when the tumor came back, she was healed in the presence of Jesus. I would love to know what Jesus did in that final year of Pam's life. She was saved for a specific mission that took one year to accomplish. What was the mission, and how many lives were given a revelation of Jesus?

Jesus is keeping that a secret for now.

REFLECT:

Is there someone in my life nearing the finish line?

Is there a secret that Jesus wants me to know?

EQUIP:

How do I look for the one nearing the finish line?

THE SECRET PLACE: If Jesus is about to reveal a secret that unlocks a heart, he is looking for worshippers to meet him in the secret place. A worshipper named David shared, "For in the time of trouble He shall hide me in His pavilion; In the secret place of His tabernacle He shall hide me; He shall set me high upon a rock" (Psalm 27:5, NKJV). As you set aside time to meet with the King, he trusts you with secrets. "We must worship our King in that secret place, that intimate time, one-on-one, as a lover of Christ. There should be times of worship that only you and the Lord will ever know about" (Darlene Zschech).

GOSPEL INTENTIONALITY: The Twins players walking by Pam did not stumble across her. They spoke into her life because of an intentionality about the gospel. During each homestand Kyle set aside time to meet with one group from the community. Every meeting included the gospel. Kyle signs baseballs with Ephesians 2:8-10. When Brian and I met with a group of college students, we talked about baseball, and then Brian talked about Jesus. After about 45 minutes one of the students said, "Are we taking too much of your time? Don't you have a game to get ready for?" Brian's response was from the heart. "This is why I play baseball. Nothing is more important than Jesus." Kyle and Brian have both been honored as All Stars, but would both testify that when a spotlight is placed in your career, you shine the light on Jesus.

LET'S PRAY:

Jesus, I don't know who is near the finish line, so I need to be near you. While the world applauds activity, I am taking the time to applaud you. If there is a secret that can unlock a heart, I am listening to your voice. As I present the gospel, I pray that every part of the old life would be dismissed by new life in Christ!

DISCUSS:

How did Paul know that he was about to finish the race?

"As for me, my life has already been poured out as an offering to God. The time of my death is near. I have fought the good fight, I have finished the race, and I have remained faithful" (2 Timothy 4:6-7).

What was Paul's reward for finishing well?

> *"And now the prize awaits me—the crown of righteousness, which the Lord, the righteous Judge, will give me on the day of his return. And the prize is not just for me but for all who eagerly look forward to his appearing"* (2 Timothy 4:8).

At the end of your life how would you feel about suffering disgrace for Jesus?

> *"The apostles left the high council rejoicing that God had counted them worthy to suffer disgrace for the name of Jesus"* (Acts 5:41).

As you near the finish line what matters the most?

> *When John Newton was nearing the finish line, he claimed that much of his memory was fading. "But I remember two things," he wrote, "that I am a great sinner, and that Christ is a great Savior."*

As I look for the one nearing the finish line, how do I become more like Jesus?

3 6

Looking For The One
WHO NEEDS KINDNESS

*"You cannot do a kindness too soon, for you
never know how soon it will be too late."*

Ralph Waldo Emerson

FORTY-FIVE MINUTES at the post office was not in anyone's schedule. The line was long, and the grumbling was understandable. When it was my turn, I thanked Karen for being so gracious despite being short of help for the day. Karen dropped her eyes and quietly said, "They're yelling at me."

A few days later, Sherrie and I walked through a farmers market in downtown Minneapolis and noticed a stand with beautiful bouquets. We thought about who we could bring flowers to on a Saturday morning. We talked about our friends and family, and then we thought of Karen. We remembered the look on her face. Moments later, we were back at the post office and noticed another long line.

We quietly asked someone at the front of the line if we could have just a moment to present the flowers and received their blessing. Sherrie gave Karen the flowers and thanked her for being so gracious on a day when people were treating her so poorly.

As Karen cried, the atmosphere shifted. A young mom stepped up and shared that she had noticed Karen's kindness. A young man declared to everyone in line, "We need more moments like this. We need to look for the best in each other." Now Karen's co-workers gathered around to share the moment. One of them held her hands.

I've thought a lot about how the atmosphere changed in the post office that day. The moment there was an act of kindness, and people in line responded with compassion and empathy. Titus 3 reminds us that when Jesus appeared, kindness appeared. "When God our Savior revealed his kindness and love, he saved us, not because of the righteous things we had done, but because of his mercy" (Titus 3:4-5).

How does kindness appear? Torii Hunter played several seasons for the Minnesota Twins. As an all-star and gold glover, his talent was one of a kind. His charisma on the field was contagious, and I frequently asked Torii to share during our chapel services. When Torii was playing for the Angels, he returned for a series in Minnesota. It was a few minutes before game time. I was visiting with a woman who had worked security at the stadium for many years. As Torii was walking to the dugout, he glanced over. Then he walked over and greeted the security guard by name. As Torri turned toward the field, something made him stop. He searched her face and asked, "Are you okay?"

She was not okay. There was a health situation, and the pressure was intense. Torii held her for a moment, then his face filled with compassion. "I am going to be praying for you."

As she watched Torii walk onto the field, she wondered aloud, "How did he know?" Torii knew because he was looking for the one. Because of that moment of kindness, the door was open to share the love of Jesus with her.

Our culture is increasingly angry. There are forces at work attempting to divide and destroy us. But do not underestimate the power of kindness. Kindness changes hearts because kindness reflects the heart of Jesus. Frederick William Faber once observed, "Kindness has converted more sinners than zeal, eloquence, or learning."

When I resist the prompting to be kind because of a critical spirit, I remember the kindness of Jesus. "Don't you see how wonderfully kind, tolerant, and patient God is with you? Does this mean nothing to you? Can't you see that his kindness is intended to turn you from your sin?" (Romans 2:4)

You might think, "It's only kindness," or "It's only flowers." But when I returned to the post office a few days later, the bouquet was still on Karen's desk.

But now, there were bouquets at every desk.

REFLECT:

Who needs my kindness?

Are there times that I struggle to be kind because I am unkind to myself?

Do I need the kindness of Jesus?

EQUIP:

How do I look for the one who needs kindness?

ON OUR KNEES: A great place to begin is by looking for the one who bothers you the most. Getting on our knees and asking Jesus to show us their heart opens our hearts to kindness. Praying blessings over them is powerful.

LOVE COVERS OVER: Is there someone in your life who is angry or has withdrawn from your circle of friends? Not every dispute needs to be processed line by line. Sometimes kindness covers the issue. "Above all, love each other deeply because love covers over a multitude of sins" (I Peter 4:8).

CONSIDER THE RICHNESS: When feeling stingy concerning kindness, consider the richness of God's mercy. "He is so rich in kindness and grace that he purchased our freedom with the blood of his Son and forgave our sins" (Ephesians 1:7).

DRESS FOR SUCCESS: In Colossians 3:12, we see a beautiful word picture: "Since God chose you to be the holy people he loves, you must clothe yourselves with kindness." As you walk with Jesus, his kindness begins to cover you. As we walk with him, we make the love of Jesus visible.

WALK WITH JESUS: To share the kindness of Jesus means you are seeing others through his eyes. That is why you notice things that others don't notice. That is why people ask, "How did you know?" Here is the secret—The only way to see people through the eyes of Jesus is to walk with Jesus. "Imitate God, therefore, in everything you do, because you are his dear children. Live a life filled with love, following the example of Christ. He loved us and offered himself as a sacrifice for us, a pleasing aroma to God" (Ephesians 5:1-2).

LET'S PRAY:

Jesus, it is a relief to declare that my life is not about me. What a joy to give my life to you and begin to see people like you see them. Instead of murmuring about the lack of kindness around me, show me specific ways to extend kindness. Help me know the language of love for people I hardly know. When I drift into a critical spirit, please remind me of your kindness to me.

DISCUSS:

What are some of the ways that God has been kind to us?

"He is so rich in kindness and grace that he purchased our freedom with the blood of his Son and forgave our sins" (Ephesians 1:7).

Who do you not want to be kind to?

"Never get tired of doing good" (2 Thessalonians 3:13).

How does kindness open a heart to the gospel?

"Again I say, don't get involved in foolish, ignorant arguments that only start fights. A servant of the Lord must not quarrel but must be kind to everyone, be able to teach, and be patient with difficult people. Gently instruct those who oppose the truth. Perhaps God will change those

> *people's hearts, and they will learn the truth. Then they will come to their senses and escape from the devil's trap. For they have been held captive by him to do whatever he wants"* (2 Timothy 2:23-26).

Do you struggle to be kind to yourself?

Do you believe in God's kindness to you?

As I look for the one who needs kindness, how am I becoming like Jesus?

Looking For The One
IN THE MIDDLE OF A FIGHT

*"They will fight you, but they will fail. For I am with you,
and I will take care of you. I, the Lord, have spoken!"*

Jeremiah 1:19

AS A GUY WHO GREW UP on a farm, city traffic sometimes makes me nervous. That is why I take public transportation whenever possible. Especially late at night. Most of the time, all is well.

On this night, I was taking the light rail from the airport to Minneapolis. The only other passenger was an older man sitting near me. The doors opened at our next stop, and a group of teenage boys swarmed into the car. Within seconds we were surrounded by guys who were yelling and cussing. I pretended to read something on my iPhone.

When there was a quiet moment, I heard the silver-haired gentleman quietly clear his throat and ask, "Do you like those shoes?" I looked up in time to see that he was speaking to the group's ringleader. The boy was wearing a brand-new pair of Nikes. As the rail car grew quiet, he responded. "Yeah, I like 'em." The man's face brightened. "Really! I've been thinking about getting a pair of those. I think I need to be walking more."

I watched in awe as this gracious man began to ask the boys about their shoes and then about their school. It was a communications masterpiece, and I was in awe.

I was also convicted.

A few weeks later, I once again stepped onto the light rail. An event had just ended at the Mall of America, and teenagers had packed the train to capacity. As the doors hissed shut, a woman began to yell.

On her end of the rail car was a group of employees from the Mall of America. On the opposite end, a group of teenagers was leaving the mall. I quickly pieced together that she had spent the day working at the Mall of America. The teenagers had spent the day making her life miserable.

She stood and shouted, "What makes you think you don't have to wait in line? What makes you think I want to pick up your garbage all day?" The kids responded with profanity, while the woman's co-workers physically restrained her.

As I began to look for my phone to find something interesting to read, I remembered the man who asked about the shoes.

Then I prayed, "Jesus, show me the one."

When there was finally a lull in the storm, I approached the woman shouting at the kids. "Tell me, what happened today?" For several minutes she gave me the details. She described the chaos and the frustration of parents standing by and watching their kids entirely out of control. As she spoke, I kept asking Jesus to show me the questions to ask. "Has this ever happened before? How long have you been working at the mall?" The longer we spoke, the quieter she became.

As I prayed, I said, "I've never had an experience like this. I can't imagine how frustrating and how helpless you felt. But I know someone who does understand. Jesus spent his life helping and serving people who mistreated him. One minute the crowds were applauding, and they turned against him the next minute. They cried out, 'Crucify him!' They spit on him." As she nodded her head, I added, "If it's okay, I would like to share how you can know Jesus."

There was a long silence, but finally, she raised her hands and boomed out, "You want to talk about Jesus? I'm down with that!" I felt every eye in the rail car focus on us.

I know there are times we don't speak up because an angry person might reject us or we don't know what to say. When you face anger or opposition, Jesus has a promise for you. "When you are arrested, don't worry about how to respond or what to say. God will give you the right words at the right time" (Matthew 10:19). If God can give you the right words during an arrest, he can certainly give you the right words when someone is angry.

By now, we were just two stops from U.S. Bank Stadium, which meant that I had about five minutes to share the good news of Jesus. I began by sharing that what happened at the Mall of America is happening worldwide. Instead of honoring each other, we mistreat one another. Instead of honor or respect, we demand our way.

"We've all messed up. But when Jesus came to earth, he gave up his rights. He came to seek us and to serve us. He came to wash our feet. Then he gave his life for us on the cross." I turned to the woman standing by my side, "He loves you and knows how you feel."

As you know, one of my favorite tools to share the gospel is The Salvation Poem. It's short, it's memorable, and packed with theology. I handed her several copies, and to my surprise, she walked around the rail car, giving them out to several of the passengers.

When she returned, I read these words:

Jesus, you died upon a cross
And rose again to save the lost
Forgive me now of all my sin
Come by my Savior, Lord, and Friend
Change my life and make it new
And help me, Lord, to live for you

I shared that if we invite Jesus in, he wants to be three things in our life: "Savior means we get a fresh start and that Jesus forgives our every sin; Lord means we surrender control of our life to him; Friend means we have the one friend who will never leave us or forsake us. Jesus wants to be all three. Your Savior, your Lord, and your best friend."

As we arrived at the train stop, I noticed the absolute calm that had descended upon that rail car. There was the unmistakable presence of God. Then I saw police cars flashing lights and a bus waiting at the U.S. Bank rail stop. As the doors opened, several officers stepped onto the train. They had been alerted to what was taking place on the rail car. But instead of a riot or a fight, they walked into the presence of God.

I said goodbye to the woman who was the spokesperson. She smiled as I told her that I would be praying for her.

I spoke to three of the officers standing nearby. They had received several phone calls and had brought the bus in case of making multiple arrests. They watched in wonder as almost every person in the car quietly left the scene.

One of the officers asked, "What happened?"

"We had a conversation about Jesus."

REFLECT:

What fight is God calling you to step into?

Do you believe that Jesus will give you the right words?

EQUIP:

How do you look for the one in the middle of a fight?

There are times when you are in the midst of angry people, and your role is to move to a place of safety. There are times when you stand and begin to speak peace.

KNOW YOUR ENEMY: No matter the person or the situation, the fight around you has a spiritual component. The real enemy in a fight is the devil. "Stay alert! Watch out for your great enemy, the devil. He prowls around like a roaring lion, looking for someone to devour. Stand firm against him, and be strong in your faith" (1 Peter 5:8-9).

CHOOSE YOUR WEAPONS: You fight with spiritual weapons because you are in a spiritual battle. Your prayers and your declaration of God's Word have divine power! "For though we walk in the flesh, we are not waging war according to the flesh. For the weapons of our warfare are not of the flesh but have divine power to destroy strongholds" (2 Corinthians 10:3-4).

CHANGE THE FOCUS: The focus instantly shifts when you approach someone in the fight, and your heart is to get to know them. When you change the subject to Jesus, his light is greater than the fight.

CONSIDER THE PROMISE: "They will fight you, but they will fail. For I am with you, and I will take care of you. I, the Lord, have spoken!" (Jeremiah 1:19)

LET'S PRAY:

Jesus, please grant us the ability to hear your voice like never before. Situations like this are impossible on our own. As we ask questions, give us deep empathy to understand the reason for their anger. Give us supernatural insight into the spiritual fight behind the physical battle. As we change the subject to Jesus, light the darkest of places with your life!

DISCUSS:

Have you ever been in the middle of a fight?

How do you know when to step into a fight?

Can you remember a time when avoiding a fight was the wrong decision?

"Now, son of man, I am making you a watchman for the people of Israel. Therefore, listen to what I say and warn them for me. If I announce that some wicked people are sure to die and you fail to tell them to change their ways, then they will die in their sins, and I will hold you responsible for their deaths. But if you warn them to repent and they

don't repent, they will die in their sins, but you will have saved yourself" (Ezekiel 33:7-9).

What is the role of a watchman on the wall?

"Meanwhile, the Lord said to me, 'Put a watchman on the city wall. Let him shout out what he sees'" (Isaiah 21:6).

How do you "Fight the good fight?"

"Fight the good fight for the true faith. Hold tightly to the eternal life to which God has called you, which you have declared so well before many witnesses" (1 Timothy 6:12).

How do you discern the spiritual forces behind a fight?

As you step into the middle of a fight, how do you become more like Jesus?

Looking For The One
IN YOUR FAMILY

*"Never worry about numbers. Help one person at a time.
And always start with the person nearest you."*

Mother Teresa

SHERRIE AND I have been blessed with six grandchildren and have talked and prayed countless times about creating one-on-one moments with each one. Our grandson Asher is eight years old, and when I discovered that he had not been to a Twins game, we circled a date on the calendar.

The Twins game had seemed like a good idea, but I could tell from the look on his face. Asher was bored. Our son Kyle tried to explain the game's rules and point out some of our favorite players. Even a hotdog did little to lift Asher's spirits. Then as we walked around, Asher noticed the mini-donuts. Now his eyes danced with excitement. As we stood in line, Asher watched the batter drop into the oil and the piping hot donuts emerging from the oil. Now it was time for a coating of sugar.

A bag of donuts was $8. The bucket of donuts was $15.

As we waited in line, I thought about the one Twins game our family had attended in the 1970s. Everyone in our family of seven knew that finances were tight. Still, somehow Mom and Dad circled a date on their calendar. We were seated in the nosebleed seats in left field, and it didn't matter that I could barely see the players or that we had no money for treats.

The Twins beat the Red Sox, and the day was magic.

As I prepared to order a bag of donuts, I remembered something else about the Red Sox game. Mom had brought along a one-gallon ice cream bucket filled with popcorn. With a family of seven, there was enough for one or two handfuls each. When Mom passed the bucket down the row, there was no complaining. You took your handful of popcorn and made it last as long as possible. I remember carefully eating the corn one kernel at a time. I remember the aroma.

As I remembered the bucket of popcorn, I ordered a bucket of donuts for Asher.

The Twins have a stadium section where you can play beanbag toss. As the donuts began disappearing, we sat on the grass and watched families tossing beanbags. Several minutes later, I heard a familiar sigh. I looked over and saw the smile on Asher's face.

When we returned to our seats, it was time for the 7th inning stretch. As we wrapped our arms around each other, we belted out "Take Me Out to the Ball Game." When the Twins came up to bat, Luis Arraez hit a home run to right field near where we were seated. As the fireworks went off, I glanced at Asher as he looked around the stadium in wonder. The game was tied in the 9th inning, but when I offered to leave early, Asher asked if we could stay until the end of the game. The Twins lost in 11 innings, but none of that mattered.

When we arrived at Kyle's home, I reached into the backseat and held Asher's hand. "Hey, Asher, I want to take a moment to pray."

"What do you want to pray about?"

"I want to thank Jesus for the game and you."

It wasn't a long or eloquent prayer, but as I thanked Jesus for Asher, I felt his hand begin to tighten. At the start of the prayer, I was holding Asher's hand. By the end of the prayer, he was holding on to me.

There are billions of people that need Jesus, but God has placed you in one family. You may go to the ends of the earth, but nothing compares to the place you call home.

As you consider your calling to serve Jesus, never forget that Jesus invited people to follow him, but he also directed followers to go home. "As Jesus was getting into the boat, the man who had been demon possessed begged to go with him. But Jesus said, 'No, go home to your family, and tell them everything the Lord has done for you and how merciful he has been.' So the man started off to visit the Ten Towns of that region and began to proclaim the great things Jesus had done for him; and everyone was amazed at what he told them" (Mark 5:18-20).

As Jesus endured the cross, he appointed John to care for his mother. "Even while he was performing the great work of redemption, Jesus was faithful to his responsibilities as a son. What an honor it was for John to take his Lord's place in Mary's life!" (Warren Wiersbe)

Taking a grandson to a Twins game doesn't build your resume, but it builds your family. You won't be thinking about money or a career at the close of life. As your family holds your hands, you will rejoice to see the love in the faces you love the most. As you close your eyes, I can hear you whisper: "I could have no greater joy than to hear that my children are following the truth" (3 John 4).

REFLECT:

Do I value a stranger's approval more than my family's love?

EQUIP:

How do I look for the one in my family?

TRIPS TO DAIRY QUEEN: If you grew up on a farm with cattle, you probably have memories of baling hay. When Dad announced it was time to bale hay, morale would quickly plummet. Baling hay was exhausting, and when it was your turn to stack the bales in the barn, it was hot and dusty. One day as we finished the last field, Dad announced that we were going to Dairy Queen. As we drove to town, visions of ice cream quickly restored our morale. Dad purchased a bag of dilly bars and thanked us for the hard work. Dad didn't say anything, but he noticed that after one dilly bar, I was still hungry. So a few days later, as we drove past Dairy Queen, Dad pulled into the parking lot. To my astonishment, Dad ordered the biggest shake they made and handed it to me. As Dad told the story, I downed the shake in record time and then sighed as I slid down the seat.

Every family faces budgets and bills and hard choices. But make sure there are memories of extravagant love. Even if there is no money, there is a way to show this kind of love.

THANKSGIVING: I grew up in a family where part of our thanksgiving tradition was to take time after the meal for each person to share a word of thanksgiving. As a teenager, one year I felt compelled to give thanks for Grandma Gertrude. As I started to speak, I suddenly began to cry. I thanked Grandma for all of her love and for not giving up when Grandpa McIver passed away so many years ago. After the meal, I walked past a bedroom as my dad wrapped his arms around Grandma and asked her to forgive him for something. They were both crying.

Your thanksgiving for the one in your family invites the presence of God.

PRAYER JOURNALS: When I was seventeen years old, our family took a trip to California, where I met my Aunt Minnie for the first time. I knew that Aunt Minnie had served as a missionary for decades, and I had heard stories about her prayer life. Moments after meeting Minnie, she showed me a spiral notebook. Then she opened the notebook to the page with my name on it. "David, I have prayed for you every day of your life. I even prayed for you as you were being knit together in your mother's womb."

Your prayers release the power of God in your family, and your prayer journal is a visual testimony that will never be forgotten.

PRAYING OVER CHAIRS: In 1996, Billy Graham hosted a crusade in Minneapolis at the Metrodome. As PraiseLive joined churches and non-profits in promoting the crusade, one of our planning meetings was at the dome. As we toured the nearly empty stadium, I noticed a team of about thirty people slowly moving from row to row. When I asked about them, one of the Graham leaders said, "They are praying over the chairs. In fact, they are praying over every single one." Since that day, when asked to share a sermon, or lead a Bible study, I pray over pews and chairs. I have prayed

over beautiful country churches and sanctuaries in
the Twin Cities that hold over 1,000 people. Then one
day before a family gathering, Jesus whispered to me.
"Pray over the chairs in your home."

LET'S PRAY:

*Jesus, I am willing to follow you and to go to the ends of the
earth. I also know my primary calling is to the ones I love
the most. Search my heart and show me any motivation to
serve a church or a distant land that is really a longing for
significance. Turn my heart toward home, and open my heart
to the ones closest to me. May our family circle be unbroken!*

DISCUSS:

How can one person influence an entire family?

*"But if you refuse to serve the Lord, then choose today
whom you will serve. Would you prefer the gods your
ancestors served beyond the Euphrates? Or will it be the
gods of the Amorites in whose land you now live? But as for
me and my family, we will serve the Lord"* (Joshua 24:15).

How did Jesus model caring for his family?

*"Standing near the cross were Jesus' mother, and his
mother's sister, Mary (the wife of Clopas), and Mary
Magdalene. When Jesus saw his mother standing there
beside the disciple he loved, he said to her, 'Dear woman,*

> *here is your son.' And he said to this disciple, 'Here is your*
> *mother.' And from then on this disciple took her into his*
> *home"* (John 19:25-27).

How does caring for our family prepare us to care for
the family of God?

> *"A deacon must be faithful to his wife, and he must manage*
> *his children and household well"* (1 Timothy 3:12).

How does looking for the one in my family make me
more like Jesus?

Are You The One?

THE LOCKER ROOM IS PACKED, and as I scan the room, I ask Jesus to show me the one. Because it is the first week of spring training, I see many faces that I do not recognize. Then as I look across the room, I see a face known around the world of baseball. The gentle face of Rod Carew. Rod's Hall Of Fame career included seven batting titles and eighteen consecutive All-Star Game selections.

The moment I saw his face, I began walking.

As I approached, Rod said, "How did you know?" As I looked somewhat puzzled, he added, "How did you know I was standing here thinking that I need to share my testimony with these guys?" I smiled at Rod, and he agreed to share his faith story at our next chapel.

It was a beautiful Sunday morning as Rod stood in the dugout. Rod shared about his career. He spoke of what it meant to be honored by the hall of fame. Rod paused, then looked down for a moment. Then he cleared his throat.

"Guys, I thought I had it all, but I was missing Jesus."

Several years later, Rod and I were sitting in the dugout, and I thanked him again for what he shared that day. We talked about his salvation and his baptism. Then Rod opened up about his heart transplant and the extra years God had given to him. Rod shared about the young man who lost his life and whose heart was beating in his chest. I told Rod that his story reminded me of God's desire to give each of us a new heart. "And I will give you a new heart, and I will put a new spirit in you. I will take out your stony, stubborn heart and give you a tender, responsive heart" (Ezekiel 36:26).

We marveled together that the cost of our new heart is the life of Jesus.

Few of us have careers that end up in a hall of fame. But we all share something with Rod. We can gain the whole world, but we can miss Jesus.

In a book about "looking for the one," I have a question for you:

"Are you the one? Are you missing Jesus?"

If you cannot remember a day of salvation, then today is a gift to you. It is not too late. "For God says, 'At just the right time, I heard you. On the day of salvation, I helped you.' Indeed, the 'right time' is now. Today is the day of salvation" (2 Corinthians 6:2).

Today is the right time to be forgiven of every sin and to know that you are going to heaven. Today is the right time to pray: "Jesus, you carried my sins on the cross so that I can be dead to sin and live for what is right. By your wounds, I am healed. Today I repent and follow you. I give my life to you and invite you to be my Savior, Lord, and Friend. Thank you for giving me a new heart."

If you have lost your first love, this is your time to pray: "Jesus, I'm weary, and I've wandered. I am far away from you, but today I am coming home. Please forgive me for taking your love for granted. Heal my heart and restore the joy of my salvation!" If this is the cry of your heart, your Father is about to welcome you home! "So he returned home to his father. And while he was still a long way off, his father saw him coming. Filled with love and compassion, he ran to his son, embraced him, and kissed him" (Luke 15:20).

If you are still hesitating, think for a moment about what is standing in your way. It might be the guilt you carry over your biggest mistake. It might be the anger toward God because of losing something precious to you. Whatever stands in your way is real, but it is not greater than the empty tomb.

Now imagine that you are standing before the empty tomb of Jesus as you read these words: "But God is so rich in mercy, and he loved us so much, that even though we were dead because of our sins, he gave us life when he raised Christ from the dead. It is only by God's grace that you have been saved!" (Ephesians 2:4-5)

Jesus whispers to you, "Come to me, all of you who are weary and carry heavy burdens, and I will give you rest" (Matthew 11:28).

As you take the first step toward Jesus, you hear his promise. "I will never fail you. I will never abandon you" (Hebrews 13:5).

As you surrender to Jesus, you are receiving your Savior, Lord, and Friend!

4 0

The Crossroad

"Do the work of an evangelist."
2 Timothy 4:5, ESV

THIS MOMENT IS A CROSSROADS in your life. You can think and pray about looking for the one, or as my dad used to say, "You can dive in with both feet."

If you are hesitant, preach God's Word to yourself. "The fruit of the righteous is a tree of life, And he who wins souls is wise" (Proverbs 11:30, NKJV).

If you are discouraged, believe God's Word. "So let's not get tired of doing what is good. At just the right time we will reap a harvest of blessing if we don't give up" (Galatians 6:9).

Yes, it is risky to stand up in the middle of a fight and speak the name of Jesus. It takes courage to say to this generation that Jesus is the way, the truth, and the life. But as you step out of your comfort zone, you are aligning your heart with God's heart. "He does not want anyone to be destroyed, but wants everyone to repent" (2 Peter 3:8-9).

If you are like me, you won't have all the answers, and you'll say the wrong thing. You'll swing and miss, and you'll be rejected. But, if you dare take the first step, you'll watch Jesus bring someone to life. You'll hear someone say, "I got it! I got it!"

And I pray that one day you'll look into the face of a new believer as they say, "That's the most beautiful thing I've ever heard."

Best of all, as the lost are found, you'll become more like Jesus.

Looking For The One
WHO _____

YOU MAY BE SURPRISED to find that the last chapter of this book has not been written. That is because the last chapter belongs to you.

The last chapter is waiting for your first story! Write it below...

For additional resources, or to share your story of looking for the one, visit: www.lookingfortheone.org

_____

_____

_____

_____

_____

_____

_____

_____

_____

_____

About the Author

DAVID MCIVER has been with the PraiseLive team since 1985 and is currently the Executive Director. He has faithfully shepherded the ministry's growth from one FM signal out of Osakis, Minnesota, to signals across Minnesota and the Dakotas. In addition, PraiseLive covers Africa and the Middle East via satellite, with over 60 FM signals rebroadcasting the worship format. People worldwide can experience Jesus at PraiseLive.org.

David is a former chapel leader with Baseball Chapel, serving the Minnesota Twins. His passion is to look for the one who needs to experience Jesus! He holds a Bachelor of Arts degree in Biblical Studies from Bethel University.

praiseLive®

Experiencing Jesus Together

**Our vision is to see every tribe and nation
experiencing Jesus together.**

In 1985, we began in rural Minnesota with a big vision. We saw people around us who had no idea who God is. They have heard about Him but have never really met Him in a personal way. In 1998, God spoke to us about changing our format to reach people with worship music, Scripture, and stories of hope. He spoke to us about broadcasting across Africa.

Now, we see this vision moving forward as people worship worldwide. Many are coming to meet Jesus!

As you listen to the praise and worship, we pray you will experience Jesus. We also pray that you will experience the joy of Jesus looking for the one through your life.

Together we help people discover and worship Jesus!

www.praiselive.org

ABOUT
SEA HARP PRESS

Sea Harp is a specialty press with one overarching aim: in the words of Andrew Murray, to "be much occupied with Jesus, and believe much in Him, as the True Vine." Our mission is twofold: to reinvigorate the Church's reading of the best of the past, and to bring out fresh editions of both today's and tomorrow's classics — all for the purpose of personal encounter with Jesus Himself.

For every piece of media we consider publishing, we ask two fundamental questions:

- Is this work entirely about the person of Jesus of Nazareth?
- Would the Early Church have thought this work worthy of sharing?

We take our name from the original Hebrew word for the Sea of Galilee—*Kinneret*: כִּנֶּרֶת: meaning "harp"—which was given because of the harp-like shape of the shoreline around which Jesus ministered. It was, in less words, a place known as the Harp-Sea.

Thank you for joining us as we walk the Way with that most wonderful Man of Galilee.

the
SEA *of*
GALILEE

WWW.SEAHARP.COM